Trailer Food Diaries COOKBOOK

Austin Edition, Volume 2

Tiffany Harelik

Serving up the American Dream one plate at a time!

AMERICAN PALATE

Published by American Palate
A Division of The History Press
Charleston, SC 29403
www.historypress.net

Cover design by Tom Kirsch Designs, LLC.

Originally published 2012

Photo credits: **Laurel Barickman** p. 172, p. 186, p. 198; **Bonnie Berry** p. 42, p. 53, p. 59, p. 60, p. 80, p. 92, p. 99, p. 113, p. 150, p. 155; **Matt Bowman** p. 188, p. 190; **Tishy Bryant** p. 13 bottom; **Rebecca Charles** p. 95; **Mary Coe** p. 48; **Enrico de Leon Jr.** p. 85, p. 153; **Connie Dowdle** p. 129; **Tiffany Harelik** p. 12, p. 14, p. 16, p. 23, p. 24, p. 27, p. 30, p. 32, p. 39, p. 46, p. 47, p. 50, p. 63, p. 104, p. 108, p. 114, p. 119, p. 136, p. 138–139, p. 142, p. 146, p. 148, p. 149, p. 156, p. 163, p. 166, p. 179; **Andy Heatwole** p. 66, p. 69, p. 71; **Robert Higgs** p. 130; **Jake Holt** p. 197; **Julia Hungerford** p. 97; **Kara Mosher** p. 118; **Ben Newman** p. 158, p. 160–161; **Suzanne Pressman** p. 117; **Sam Rhodes** p. 34, p. 90; **Schelly Schaefer** p. 91; **Margo Sivin** p. 40, p. 180; **Snap Pod** p. 140; **Ryan Sumagaysay** p. 21; **Laurie Virkstis** p. 101, p. 145; **Aimee Wenske** p. 103, p. 111.

Manufactured in the United States

ISBN 978.1.60949.856.6

Library of Congress CIP data applied for.

Contents

Sauces

San Marcos: A Day Trip to the Trailers

Sides

Handhelds

Dinners

Acknowledgements

The *Trailer Food Diaries Cookbook* and projects are dependent on many people. I am grateful for my role in compiling and narrating and would like to acknowledge with deep appreciation those who made the *Trailer Food Diaries* second edition of Austin possible: the trailer food vendors with their rich personal histories and recipes, my supportive family, Maurine Winkley, Tom Kirsch (Tom Kirsch Design), the Gemini Moon Writers' Group (Deborah Mastellato, Connie Quillen, Mollie Staffa, Kriss Kovach, Elizabeth Decker, Brooke Carter), Bonnie Berry (photography), Karen Frost, Stewart Ramser and Bob Gentry. To The History Press, thank you for your enthusiasm and commitment to this series.

Introduction
The Crawl That Started It All, Y'all

Before I was writing the *Trailer Food Diaries*, I was a single mom working at a job that was less than fulfilling. After one year of working for the company, I was offered a nickel raise. A few short months after that, I decided, with the help of my parents, to embark on a new chapter. In December 2009, I quit my job with no savings account, no hope of unemployment assistance and no idea what I really wanted to do with myself.

Come February 2010, I began noticing more and more food trailers pop up in my hometown of Austin, Texas. Some girlfriends invited me on a trailer food crawl that month. We hit up Odd Duck, but they were closed for lunch. We found Lulu B's, but they were closed that day. We found Izzoz and enjoyed some authentic tacos. We found Gourdough's and sat by the curb of South Lamar to share some oversized doughnuts along with a twelve-pack of beer. Looking at one another under the red umbrellas, everyone was happy, but the crawl left something to be desired. Some of the trailers we really wanted to try weren't open, some we couldn't find and some we found by chance.

I decided this type of rogue organization just wouldn't do. This was Austin, after all, and there ought to be some local figure to represent the incredibly hip gourmet menus these trailer-chefs were serving. I Googled, I Facebooked, I Tweeted. No one. I started a blog with no background or basic understanding of blogging. All of a sudden, I had forty pageviews, and they weren't all me. The views kept increasing as I kept reviewing the trailers and sharing their stories.

What made my writing so successful was that I had a different take on the trailers than the average foodie blog. I was interested in promoting their menus and locations, but I was *more* interested in how they started their trailer food business. My background in psychology made me ask questions like "What makes an attorney quit his practice to start a food truck?" or "How did this immigrant start his life here with only ninety dollars in his pocket?" I realized I was on the same journey as many of the food truck entrepreneurs. We were all pursuing the American dream, one plate at a time. Each of us was looking for fulfilling work, trying to find something to make us proud at the end of the day.

By May 2010, I had the travel bug and started moving about the country. One of my journeys led me to Honduras, where Shay Spence, my digging partner, became interested in what I was up to with the *Trailer Food Diaries*. "You gotta tell my dad what you're doing. He just bought a food trailer and is selling his hot sauce out of it." So after a week of manual labor under the Honduran sun, having ridden uphill in an open cattle trailer in the rain, having sat in Houston for an all-day delay and ultimately landing in Austin surrounded by a cloud of rank jungle stench, I stuck out my hand to meet Shay's dad, Roy Spence, founding partner at GSD&M advertising agency, one of the largest and most well-respected agencies in the Southwest. Roy ignored my hand and pulled me in for a hug. After a brief sentence explaining my vision for the *Trailer Food Diaries*, he invited me to his office downtown to brainstorm ideas. What Roy taught me in that initial meeting was one of the most important lessons I've learned since I began writing this series. He told me three things he learned from his father, which were also part of the Royito's (his hot sauces) mission:

1. Be kind to everyone; you never know what someone is going through.
2. Keep it simple (which, he'll tell you, he failed miserably at).
3. Don't do mild! (That's in life but has double meaning with the salsa.)

Another group of friends introduced me to C3 Presents, the local production company responsible for such festivals as the Austin City Limits Music Festival, Lollapalooza Music Festival in Chicago and beyond. We had our initial meeting in May 2010, and by November 2010, one day before my thirtieth birthday, we co-produced the first annual Gypsy Picnic trailer food festival. Over twenty thousand people came to try food from thirty trailers. The following year, over thirty thousand people came to eat from close to forty trailers. It was at that second picnic that I launched the *Trailer Food Diaries Cookbook* series.

My vision for the series remains the same: multiple editions of cookbooks in each city where it makes sense, along with some special editions focusing on a niche food topic (vegetarian, sweets, tacos, etc.). My intention in writing the series is to inspire people not only to try some great new food and to eat locally but also to inspire people to take a look at their own pursuit of the American dream.

Something else Roy taught me over the years in regard to our economy is the importance of supporting mom and pop businesses. "Our country was built on small," he'll say, smiling, "and I'm working my way down the corporate ladder." We can support our local economy through the trailer food movement and help hardworking families achieve their dreams. It is possible to have a job you love while also paying your bills and putting money into savings. This has been the underlying story behind each of the personalities, recipes and histories of the *Trailer Food Diaries*.

Drinks

Carribbean Carrot Latte
Sun Farm Kitchen

Cherry Lemonade
Cow Bell's

Gingerspice Ale
Schmaltz

Gypsy Juice
The Gypsy Kit

Mango Peach Rosemary Ginger Cooler
Chi'Lantro

Moroccan Tea
The Flying Carpet

Raspberry Passion Fruit Tea with Lemon Raspberry Ice Cubes
Fresh Off the Truck

Strawberry Basil Smoothie
MamboBerry

The Founders Fav
Blenders and Bowls

The Healthy Hulk
Blenders and Bowls

The Inner Warrior
ChocoSutra

Carribbean Carrot Latte

Courtesy of Sun Farm Kitchen

Healthy, cool and smooth, this drink is a refreshing treat.
Yield: 1 serving.

1 part carrot juice

1 part coconut or almond milk

dash of angustura bitters

dash of cinnamon

dash of nutmeg

• Mix together with a spoon until blended. Serve on ice with whipped cream and mint garnish.

Cherry Lemonade

Courtesy of Cow Bell's

The sweet and sour flavors of summer make a beautiful picnic pitcher.
Yield: 2 quarts.

6 large lemons

2 quarts water

1 cup grenadine

1 cup sugar

cherries

• Fill a large pitcher with 2 quarts of cold water. Cut lemons in half and squeeze juice into the pitcher. Use a strainer to clean out seeds and save the pulp.

• Add pulp, grenadine and sugar. Stir well, then serve in a tall glass with extra crushed ice. Place a cherry on top to garnish.

Gingerspice Ale

Courtesy of Schmaltz

A citrus fresh tonic that uses cloves, cinnamon and ginger. Yield: 4–6 drinks.

6 cups water

1 cup fresh ginger root, grated

1 cup sugar

4 teaspoons dried whole cloves

4 cinnamon sticks

1 lemon

1 lime

1 orange

- Bring 6 cups of water to a boil.

- While water is boiling, grate fresh ginger root. Add ginger root, sugar, cloves and cinnamon sticks to a big bowl and pour boiling water over. Stir and steep for one hour or more.

- Juice each citrus fruit and add to your mixture. Strain through cheesecloth.

- This tea can be added to kombucha (1:4) for flavoring or to sparkling water (1:1) for a delicious and refreshing beverage.

Gypsy Juice

Courtesy of The Gypsy Kit

A favorite drink around the porch.

12 (12-ounce) Lonestar light beers

2 (12-ounce) cans frozen limeade

6 ounces triple sec

12 ounces Jose Cuervo Silver

• Mix all ingredients and serve over ice. Garnish with cayenne salt–dusted lime wheel.

The Gypsy Kit, Tagan and Chris Couch

"Without struggle, there is no progress!" is the tattoo Tagan got right before she opened the Gypsy Kit. Tough grit runs in the family, as both of Tagan's grandmothers owned small town cafés and her great-grandmother is the one who taught her how to make coleslaw and bake pies and cakes. She is inspired by their persistence and determination to make a living for their families even during the toughest of times.

Tagan was trying to wait until her husband returned from Afghanistan before opening their trailer-dream. But full of her own determination, when the perfect location became available, she felt like she needed to make a move before losing the opportunity. So she purchased a 1979 Shasta Freedom Trailer from a family friend, rebuilt it to suit her needs and opened her doors for business.

"The name The Gypsy Kit came from the fact that everyone always called me the Kitchen Gypsy. I cannot stand to stay in a restaurant [where] a menu never changes," shares Tagan.

Mango Peach Rosemary Ginger Cooler

Courtesy of Chi'Lantro

A light, refreshing drink that is easy to make.

4 cups mango nectar

4 cups peach puree

2 rosemary sprigs

4 cups of ginger ale

• Combine all ingredients, drain and serve chilled.

Moroccan Tea

Courtesy of The Flying Carpet

On any afternoon or morning everywhere in Morocco, people are preparing or drinking tea. It is often referred to as the Moroccan whiskey. Teapots are brought out in houses and on street corners; some are fancy and elegant, but most are worn, well loved and served next to mismatched glasses. It is a part of Moroccan life as dear to the people as the conversations and relationships that accompany it. Note: Traditional Moroccan tea is very sweet by American standards.

6 cups boiling water

1 ½ tablespoons Chinese gunpowder green tea

1 extra large bunch of spearmint

4–6 tablespoons turbinado sugar

• Boil water; put small amount into teapot, swirl around and then dump. This is to clean the teapot of any residue.

• Once the teapot is empty, put in gunpowder green tea and spearmint. Next, pour the remainder of the boiling water over the mint and tea. Finally, add sugar and stir. Cover and let steep for three to five minutes. Serve hot.

The Flying Carpet, Maria and Abderrahim Souktouri

Against all odds, Abderrahim "Abdu" Souktouri won the lottery for United States citizenship when he was twenty-seven years old. Leaving his street-food business selling roasted nuts in Morocco, he arrived in Austin with ninety dollars in his pocket. He soon met the love of his life, his wife, Maria. After their son Talib was born, Maria quit her job as a paralegal to stay home with their baby while Abdu maintained his job at the Dell factory. Somewhere between dirty diapers and long days at the factory, the couple decided to do something they enjoyed that was just for them.

Former Barton Springs lifeguard Maria tells it like this: "We've always entertained and been foodies; having parties for thirty to forty people at our house is not a strange thing. People rant and rave about our food, and we'd talked about what it would be like to open a restaurant ever since we first got together fifteen years ago. But we knew enough to be scared. When we thought about opening the trailer, we also came up with plans B and C. Plan B was to sell the trailer. Plan C was to move to Morocco. But there were so many confirmations once we started the business, and I realized the house, the biggest thing we'll ever

buy, even if we lose it, it doesn't change who we are. Life isn't a dress rehearsal; it's now. What are we waiting for? The trailer was something we could financially and logistically do."

Maria and Abdu Souktouri are the heart and soul of The Flying Carpet, with cultures as bold and brilliant as the food they are serving. The Moroccan Lemon Butter and Olive Chicken with French Fries is one of their family favorites. This chicken dish is often served with a cucumber/tomato salad, French fries and bread to sop up the sauce. But it's The Moroccan that is their bestseller. Starting with a pure bread made of flour, salt and water, they pour a slow-cooked tomato sauce that includes peeled tomatoes, spices, onions and garlic. Three fingers of beef are laid on top of the sauce, and a fried egg is then added as a final touch.

Raspberry Passion Fruit Tea with Lemon Raspberry Ice Cubes

Courtesy of Fresh Off the Truck

A pretty party drink you can use year-round. The baking soda softens the natural tannins that cause an acid or bitter taste to tea. Yield: 2 quarts.

4 cups boiling water, reserve 2 cups

2 cups granulated sugar

3 pints fresh raspberries, reserve 1 pint for ice cubes

pinch baking soda

4 bags Tazo Passion Fruit Tea

2 bags Lipton black tea

1 cup cold water

lemonade

ice cube tray

lemon and raspberry for garnish

• Heat 2 cups water, sugar and raspberries in a small pot until syrupy. Puree. Put baking soda and tea bags in a pot and add the boiling water. Cover and let steep for 7 to 10 minutes. Remove the tea bags, being careful not to break them. Combine the cold water, tea mixture and raspberry syrup to sweetness.

For the Ice Cubes:

• Get ice tray and put 1 or 2 raspberries in each slot. Pour lemonade into ice tray, freeze and use for teas.

• Cut lemon slices and use them and leftover raspberries to garnish.

Strawberry Basil Smoothie

Courtesy of MamboBerry

1 cup ice

4 ounces tart frozen yogurt

1 cup fresh or frozen strawberries

4 ounces apple juice

2 ounces orange juice

1 tablespoon fresh lemon juice

5 large fresh basil leaves

sweeten to taste if desired

- Add ingredients to blender. Blend. Pour. Drink.

MamboBerry, Rena Willis

Rena Willis was living in Dallas when she decided she needed a career and location change. "I'm very entrepreneurial, graduated from business school, always wanted to open a business and am a complete foodie…so what better opportunity than to open a food truck in one of the best cities around?" she shares.

With her brother and sister-in-law's help, she created an eccentric menu that offers a variety of homemade, healthy choices. "We're the only place in town where you can find a Strawberry Basil Smoothie, a true Greek Frappe, Sweet Potato Pecan and Chipotle Mushroom Tamales, a Bacon Croissant Sandwich with Homemade Peach Jam, Aged Brie and Fresh Basil," shares Rena. Their smoothies are made with fresh fruits and no added sugars, powders or syrups. However, their Fried Kool-Aid has been a top seller and received much attention from the media.

"The Orange Creamsicle Smoothie tastes just like the Flintstones push-up pops from when I was little. It gets my taste buds and childhood memories churning every time. My favorite food item is the MamboBerry Salad. It's grilled turkey breast, peppered bacon, gorgonzola, red onion, walnuts, dried cranberries and warm diced peaches all served over a bed of organic mixed greens with balsamic vinaigrette or light raspberry vinaigrette. Yum," Rena explains.

The 1995 Chevy step van was a Fed Ex truck originally. It drives well and gets them to all the hungry people at local events. Celebrity guests include Colt McCoy and his wife, Eve 6 and Lance Armstrong.

The Founders Fav

Courtesy of Blenders and Bowls

Blenders and Bowls founded their food truck menu based on a love for açaí. This delicious drink is easy to make and so good for you.

1 Sambazon Original Açaí Smoothie Pack

8 ounces apple juice

3 or 4 medium to large frozen strawberries

3 ounces frozen banana

• Combine ingredients in a blender. Blend until smooth.

The Healthy Hulk

Courtesy of Blenders and Bowls

A punch that would make Popeye proud.

7 ounces apple juice

1 ounce orange juice

2 cups spinach (about two handfuls)

1 small cube of ginger root skinned

3 or 4 medium to large frozen strawberries

3 ounces frozen banana

• Combine apple juice and orange juice with frozen ingredients in a blender. Blend until smooth.

Blenders and Bowls, Kara Jordan and Erin Downing

"Erin and I both spent time in Hawaii, and while we lived there, grabbing an açaí bowl after surfing became the norm. When we moved to Austin, it was shocking that in such a healthy place there was nowhere to get açaí! We took matters into our own hands, and the rest is history. Blenders and Bowls is Austin's first açaí café and mobile food truck," says Kara Jordan.

The Chill Berry has been a favorite of Kara's and a bestseller right from the start. It is a super thick blend of açaí and apple juice topped with hemp granola, strawberry, blueberry, goji berry and drizzled with local Round Rock Honey. The Dream Boat is their most popular "blender" and combines vanilla almond milk with açaí. Erin's favorite is the Sesher: açaí blend loaded with peanut butter, chocolate hemp milk, blueberries and bananas. It's topped with bananas, cashews, cacao nibs, raisins and local honey.

Two best friends from Santa Barbara, California, never dreamed they would be opening a food truck, but when push came to shove, they quit their day jobs and went full steam ahead to get Blenders and Bowls up and running in a few short months. "We came up with the idea at the start of April, bought the truck in June, had our first event in July. It was a very quick execution with a go-getter mindset," says Erin Downing.

Kara says, "Neither of us ever thought we'd be working for ourselves in the food industry! We had both been waitresses before, but it was nothing compared to what we do now. We wanted to do something that had never been done before in Austin, and we wanted to get started right away. Owning a food truck was the answer for us. There were no huge hurdles into entry, start-up costs were low and owning a mobile truck would give us the ability to be in more than just one location."

The Inner Warrior

Courtesy of ChocoSutra

This is a good pre- or post-workout drink. It supplies the body with quick and sustained energy. Add whey protein or colostrum to further enhance it for muscle repair and building.

10 ounces Gynostemma tea (Spring Dragon Longevity Tea from Dragon Herbs)

1 ounce raw cacao paste (Cacao Liquor)

1 tablespoon raw cacao powder

1–2 teaspoons virgin coconut oil, cold pressed

1 tablespoon hemp seeds

1 tablespoon chia seeds, soaked in ¼ cup to ½ cup of lukewarm water for about 20 minutes, to form a gel (The seed will soak up the water and will swell. A gel-like membrane will form around it, and it will become suspended in the water.)

1–2 tablespoons raw local honey

1 teaspoon maca powder

½ teaspoon cordyceps powder (Can be omitted if you don't have it, but it is powerful in this drink to enhance energy and stamina. It is also considered a lung tonic and is beneficial for the lung meridian. It's incredibly beneficial for athletes because it boosts core energy.)

pinch of salt

- The base of this drink will need to be made while warm, as the fats of the cacao paste and coconut oil need to be melted to fully emulsify into the water.

- Brew the tea, and while still hot, combine the cacao paste, powder and coconut oil together in a blender and blend until it's well incorporated. This is the base. It can be used to make any sort of combination of ingredients to your liking.

- For this recipe, add the hemp seeds, chia gel, honey, maca, cordyceps and salt and blend again. Blend long enough to make sure the hemp seeds and chia seeds are nicely blended. You may need to use a strainer to strain out the seeds if you don't have a high-powered blender. Also, you may want to add more honey, if you like it on the sweeter side.

- For a cold drink instead, the base can be chilled down, then blended with the rest of the ingredients and ice. You could also blend ice into the hot base, but most likely it'll come out warmer than you might want. So that's why I recommend cooling the base in the refrigerator first.

ChocoSutra, Delia (Snoopy) Storey and Richard Kreuzburg

"We work from the idea of food being medicine. The famous quote by Hippocrates, 'Let food be thy medicine and medicine be thy food,' is the basis of our concept. Not only does our product taste good, but it makes you feel good," says Richard Kreuzburg.

Delia (Snoopy) Storey and Richard Kreuzburg developed the ChocoSutra concept over a few years. Richard's interest in chocolate led him to study the lore, history and science behind it. "In its pure state, I found, it can be a very potent food," says Richard. He talks about chocolate as a food, not an indulgence or treat. Soon, he began experimenting with other healthy, nontraditional superfoods. Snoopy added a very complementary and different side to what Richard had started. "We're both kind of nerdy about metaphysical-type stuff. So she, especially, is always checking the energetics of things," shares Richard.

"When we first opened, I expected to have a lot of customers that are younger, in their twenties or thirties. We actually have quite a few loyal customers that are much older. I've since realized our drinking chocolate is more like sipping a fine wine or an exceptional whiskey. A well-developed taste in a person allows them to truly appreciate the chocolate and flavor profiles," shares Richard.

The chocolate bonbons are the bestseller, mainly because they are small and people buy multiple at a time. The bonbons are flavored primarily with essential oils but sometimes spices such as saffron or turmeric.

Richard's favorite menu item is the Inner Sage. "It's a chocolate elixir that combines Chinese and ayurvedic herbs with an unsweetened chocolate base. Brown gold, in my opinion. It's pretty intense, but I think it's really nice. It's a combo of reishi mushroom, shilajit, cherry concentrate and goji berries in our chocolate base. It's better warm, but on these hot Austin summer days, it's really nice cold," he explains.

"Our biggest hurdle is the education to our customers about what we do. Most people see the word chocolate and assume they know all about it. So we get overlooked a lot as being 'just chocolate.' Then once someone tries it, there is almost always a look of surprise on their face. Usually it's a positive surprised look, meaning they really enjoy it and it's not anything like they expected, though occasionally we get someone that doesn't care for it. But once they've tried it, it's really easy to talk with them about how different our chocolate is from any store-bought chocolate. There's so much intention behind our product to be really high quality. We use a lot of ingredients that are unfamiliar to most people. I've actually taken the ingredients of our elixirs off the menu so people would stop getting nervous about not liking something because they didn't know what it was. I freely tell them if they ask though, but most people don't ask unless they have some dietary restrictions," Richard explains.

Austin Trailers Then and Now

When Austin City Limits Music Festival was started, the producers leaned on the wisdom of Chef Jeff Blank of Hudson's on the Bend. Jeff became the liaison of the food court, helping create dishes that were truly reflective of good Austin cuisine. "We are just having low-brow fun with a high-brow attitude," Jeff will tell you. His first menu item for the festival became an iconic dish that any ACL-er longs for each year: the Hot and Crunchy Mighty Cone. Consisting of mouthwatering hot and crunchy fried chicken wrapped sideways in a cone-shaped tortilla and topped with mango-jalapeño slaw and ancho paint, the Mighty Cone will make you a believer in street food cuisine. Understandably, people demanded a Mighty Cone that was available year-round. But this wasn't the type of cuisine Jeff could serve at his high-end restaurant off Lake Travis. So he opened one of Austin's first iconic food trailers. (Note: Jeff's recipe for the Mighty Cone is available in *Trailer Food Diaries Cookbook: Austin Edition, Volume I*).

A few other founding fathers of the trailer food world began popping up: Flip Happy Crepes, Torchy's Tacos and Hey Cupcake. By 2010, Austin was home to a few hundred food trailers, with over three thousand folks applying for permits to own and operate mobile food businesses.

Appetizers

Fried Pickles
SoCo to Go

Guacamole Cacao
ChocoSutra

Green Chile Hummus
The Fat Cactus

Okra Fritters with Peach Salsa
Seedling Truck

Scallion Pancake with Soy Dipping Sauce
Fresh Off the Truck

Patatas Bravas (Spicy Fried Potatoes)
Tapas Bravas

Sweet Po Tater Tots with Feta-Ranch Dipping Sauce
Dock and Roll Diner

WhataQueso with Chips
WhaTaTaco

Wurst Tex Truffle Fries
Wurst Tex

Fried Pickles

Courtesy of SoCo to Go

Frying pickles is easier than you think, and they make for a fun appetizer.
Yield: 6 servings.

1 cup flour

1 cup cracker meal (or saltine crackers, finely crushed)

4 teaspoons Tony Cachere's seasoning

2½ teaspoons cayenne pepper

2 eggs

⅔ cup milk

50 kosher dill pickle chips, crinkle cut

canola oil for frying

- Combine flour, cracker meal (or crushed crackers) and seasonings. Mix well to incorporate.

- Combine eggs and milk in separate bowl; beat well.

- Dredge pickles in breading, then egg/milk mixture, then breading again.

- Heat oil in fryer to approximately 360 degrees. Fry 3 to 4 minutes until golden brown. Drain. Serve with your favorite ranch dressing and enjoy!

Guacamole Cacao

Courtesy of ChocoSutra

Cacao nibs are a unique addition to this tasty appetizer.
Yield: 3–4 servings.

2 medium avocados, slightly firm

1 habanero pepper, minced

1 clove garlic, minced

1 lime

⅛–¼ teaspoon whole cumin seed

1 tablespoon extra-virgin olive oil, cold pressed

3 tablespoons cilantro, chopped, to taste

sea salt to taste

2 tablespoons organic cacao nibs

• Cut the avocados in half and remove the seeds. Take your knife and cut diagonally both ways into the flesh of the avocado in a crisscross pattern so that when you scoop it out with a spoon, it is already cut into cubes. I like to leave the avocado chunky for texture. You can mash it if you'd like for a smoother guacamole.

• Mix in as much of the habanero as you can handle, followed by the garlic, juice of the lime, cumin and olive oil, plus cilantro and sea salt to taste. Give it all a good mix and check the seasoning to make sure it tastes good.

• Scoop it all in your serving dish and sprinkle the cacao nibs on top. You can also mix some cacao nibs into the guacamole, but make sure you have enough to garnish the top. Serve it with blue corn chips or your favorite dipper.

Green Chile Hummus

Courtesy of The Fat Cactus

The New Mexican green chile is the star of this popular dip.
Yield: 1 quart.

3–4 medium-sized garlic cloves

1 jalapeño (roughly chopped)

1 (29-ounce) can garbanzo beans or 2 (15-ounce) cans, drained and rinsed

1 tablespoon tahini

½ teaspoon cumin

salt and pepper

juice of 1 lime

½ cup water

½ cup extra virgin olive oil

1 cup mild chopped green chiles (if using hot, omit jalapeño and only use ½ cup)

2 teaspoons sambal oelek (optional, but I like and suggest it)

¼ cup packed chopped cilantro

- Place garlic and jalapeño in food processor and run until finely chopped. Add beans, tahini, cumin, salt, pepper and lime juice and process.

- Begin adding water until a thick puree forms but is still pretty tight. Next drizzle in oil. Paste should be smooth but still a little "tighter" than normal hummus.

- Taste and adjust salt, pepper and lime juice if necessary. Add green chiles, sambal and cilantro and pulse until combined but not really blended. Alternatively, you can remove hummus to a bowl and fold in chiles and cilantro to keep from over processing.

- Serve with frybread, pita, tortilla chips or fresh veggies.

The Fat Cactus, Chris Howell and Courtney Jones

With several years in the service industry behind their belts, Courtney and Chris thought opening a food trailer was the perfect solution to finding a way to showcase Chris's unique southwestern menu. "It took about two years to get from, 'Hey, you wanna open a food trailer?' to 'We finally did it, we're open!'" shares Chris.

With his chef father and foodie mother, Chris grew up in restaurants and around good food. "I was always drawn to the flavors, colors and ingredients of the Southwest. They are heavily represented in my cooking style. Both my parents have lived in New Mexico or Arizona and have given me ample opportunity to travel and taste the foods of the region.

"After driving through New Mexico and Arizona on a roadtrip with Courtney, we realized that nearly every little town we passed through had a little old lady in a trailer making frybread tacos. After eating a few, we thought, 'No one in Austin is doing this that we know of; maybe this is the concept.' We wanted to respect the traditions and the past but also respect cooking in general by trying to push the frybread forward and applying different concpts and preparations. It really is a tasty canvas for just about anything: tacos, pizzas, sausages, paninis, desserts—we do it.

"We love each other and we love food (especially the food we make). I've learned so much in the kitchen trying to make the best possible food for her. Even though we've never been rich, I've always wanted her to eat better than anyone else. Without her encouragement, love, support and gifts for my (now our) kitchen, I would never be the cook I am, and The Fat Cactus would never have been."

The Foghorn frybread pizza is Chris's favorite thing on the menu. It has cilantro–pumpkin seed pesto, chile-roasted chicken, red onions, goat cheese and roasted pepitas. Customers love the OG Taco, which contains ground beef sautéed with onions and garlic, borracho beans, shredded colby jack, lettuce, tomato and their choice of green or red New Mexico chile sauce.

Their customers from the Navajo reservations were the least expected. "There are more Navajo in Austin and Texas than you would think, and to hear from them that our food is awesome means the world to us," shares Chris.

Okra Fritters with Peach Salsa

Courtesy of Seedling Truck

This dish makes for a great southern snack during a late Indian summer when both peaches and okra are in season.

Okra Fritters:

3 strips bacon

1 medium yellow onion, diced

2 cloves garlic, minced

1 tablespoon olive oil

2 pounds fresh okra

2 tablespoons white wine

3 cups cornmeal

¼ cup water

salt and pepper, to taste

sour cream, as desired for flavorful garnish

• In sauté pan over medium heat, sweat the bacon, onion and garlic in olive oil until soft, 4 to 5 minutes. The idea is to draw the water out of the ingredients to make them transparent without making anything crispy or changing color. Add sliced okra to pan and sauté until lightly golden, 8 to 10 minutes.

• Deglaze pan with white wine and set aside to cool. If you are new to deglazing, the idea is to pour the white wine into the pan full of hot ingredients to get the flavorful bits off the bottom of the pan. You'll want to scrape the bottom to get all of the ingredients loose. This process takes less than a minute. Be careful: if you have too high of a heat, the alcohol will create a flame. You do not want a flame when deglazing.

• In large bowl, mix the okra mixture with cornmeal, water, salt and pepper until you get the consistency of thick peanut butter. Spoon medium-sized dollops onto a nonstick pan on medium heat with the olive oil and cook 2 to 3 minutes on each side.

Peach Salsa:

3 ripe peaches, diced, leave skin on

1 red onion, medium diced

1 bunch cilantro, chopped

1 lime, cut in half to squeeze

1 tablespoon peach vinegar

• Combine peach, red onion, cilantro and a squeeze of lime. Sauté salsa in sauté pan until the fruit becomes soft. Add the peach vinegar, allowing to cook down for 1 to 2 minutes or as needed.

Serving the Fritters:

• Top cooked fritters with peach salsa and a little sour cream if desired.

Scallion Pancake with Soy Dipping Sauce

Courtesy of Fresh Off the Truck

Try making this Asian-themed pancake for an appetizer.

3 cups all-purpose flour

kosher salt in a ramekin, to taste

1½ cups warm water

1 bunch scallions

2 cups canola or vegetable oil

• Sift flour in a big bowl and add a pinch or two of salt. Mix well. Add water slowly to the flour and knead well until a smooth dough forms, about 10 minutes. If the dough is dry, add more water. Rest the dough for 30 minutes with a damp cloth covering it.

• Slice scallions diagonally on a bias, about ¼-inch thick.

• After dough has rested, separate the dough into equal portions—about 2 to 3 ounces of dough. Roll each portion into a ball and roll it out into a disc with a rolling pin. Dust with flour if needed. Using a brush, brush oil onto the disc. Sprinkle salt and scallions to desire.

• Roll the disc up from the bottom into a cylinder. Then coil the cylinder to make a snail and tuck the tail in between the other layers to create a secure knot. Press down on the snail and roll the snail into a flat pancake. Repeat for the rest of the dough. Add some oil to a frying pan and pan fry until golden brown on each side.

Soy Dipping Sauce:

½ cup soy sauce

¼ cup hot water

1 tablespoon sugar

½ tablepoon vinegar

1 teaspoon Sriracha sauce

• Combine all in a sauce pot and simmer gently for about 1 minute. Garnish with scallions.

Patatas Bravas (Spicy Fried Potatoes)

Courtesy of Tapas Bravas

Also known as Patatas a la Brava or simply Bravas, this is one of Spain's most definitive tapas. Bravas—fierce—refers to the spicy tomato sauce, and this is one of the only spicy dishes that you will find in Spain. These can be found everywhere, but most people go in groups to tapas bars that specialize in Bravas; top them off with a garlicky ajoaceite and you have a Spanish classic. Yield: 4–6 servings (or about 1 potato per serving).

4–6 large white potatoes, about 10–12 ounces each

olive oil or vegetable oil for frying

salt

Salsa Brava (spicy tomato sauce, recipe below)

Ajoaceite (fresh garlic mayonnaise, recipe below)

parsley if desired, for garnish

• Peel and cut potatoes into ¾-inch chunks, then rinse, drain and pat dry with paper towels. Fry potatoes at 350°F for approximately 3 minutes and allow to cool and drain over the pan or fryer for 2 minutes. Fry again for 3 minutes longer, until golden brown, and drain over paper towels.

• Lightly toss with a dash of salt and serve individual portions or a group platter. Arrange the potatoes in each serving dish and drizzle with Salsa Brava, then top with Ajoaceite, or serve the sauces on the side, garnish with chopped parsley and eat with toothpicks.

Salsa Brava (Spicy Tomato Sauce):

1 tablespoon olive oil

3 garlic cloves, chopped

1 medium onion, chopped

2 teaspoons smoked Spanish paprika

1 teaspoon ground cumin

1½ tablespoons dried Chile de Arbol powder

1 can (15 ounces) peeled plum tomatoes, chopped, with liquid

1 tablespoon white vinegar

1 teaspoon sugar

½ teaspoon salt

• Heat the oil in a medium-sized saucepan over medium heat. Add the garlic and onion and cook until soft but not browned, about 5 minutes. Add paprika, cumin and red pepper. Stir and cook until fragrant, about 1 minute.

• Add the tomatoes and their liquid and ½ cup water and bring to a simmer. Simmer uncovered until the tomatoes have cooked down, about 15 to 20 minutes, stirring occasionally. Add the vinegar, sugar and salt and cook 3 minutes longer.

• Remove from the heat and allow to cool for five minutes, then puree in a blender. Allow to cool before serving. If made ahead, warm slightly before serving.

Ajoaceite (Garlic Mayonnaise):

Ajoaceite is Spain's potent garlic mayonnaise, also known by its Catalán name, Allioli. In Cataluña and along the eastern coast, people are convinced that everything tastes better with ajoaceite, from paella to seafood, grilled meats and vegetables. First documented in first-century Rome, the name literally means "garlic oil," and authentic allioli Catalán is made with nothing more. The oil is painstakingly whisked, drop by drop, into a paste of mortar-pounded garlic. This is the recipe more commonly used in Spain today. It simplifies and demystifies this classic sauce.

10 cloves garlic, to taste

1 teaspoon salt

1 pasteurized egg

1 tablespoon lemon juice

1 cup olive oil

• In a blender, roughly mix the garlic, salt, egg and lemon juice. Gradually, with the motor running, slowly incorporate the oil—drop by drop at first, then gradually in a slow trickle or stream. Scrape down the sides of the blender a couple times as you go so all the garlic is well blended until you have a smooth and thickened sauce.

• Transfer the sauce to a serving bowl. The ajoaceite is best after it sits out at room temperature for an hour and is even better if allowed to rest overnight, covered, in the refrigerator. It will keep that way for up to 3 days.

Tapas Bravas, Jed Holdredge and Alex Hord

"It's been a lot of hard work getting my food truck started, but it could not be a more fun and more rewarding business to be in. Austin has the best street food in the country, and to be a part of that culture and represent Austin is an honor that I take very seriously," shares Jed.

Originally from Athens, Texas, Jed Holdredge was a very finicky eater and refused to eat most dishes (even French fries). However, he was lucky in that his family hosted an exchange student from Spain in high school (they are still friends to this day). "Once I graduated, I moved to Valencia with his family and experienced how the food and culture are inseparable. When I fell in love with Spanish culture, food came with it, and I learned how the most simple dishes at home and the impossibly complex and inventive dishes in high-end restaurants all make up the Spanish palate. While studying Spanish language and literature at home and in the classroom, I also learned how to cook in the family home... and how to eat out at the tapas bars with friends," says Jed.

The Tapas Bravas trailer was opened because Jed and business partner Alex Hord saw an opportunity for his cuisine to be highlighted in the niche market of food trucks. Jed elaborates, "The Austin food trailer business is exploding and is the best way to get authentic, quality dishes to the Foodie population. With a casual attitude, tapas are a perfect fit. Where else can you get Rabbit Terrine, Spanish Tortilla and fresh Churros in a backyard eatery? The cost savings mean we can get local foods and make everything by hand and in many cases fresh to order."

One of the most popular items on the Tapas Bravas menu is the croquetas; it's a staple Tapa all over Spain and one of the most labor-intensive to make. The filling of soft bechamel, chicken, Jamón Serrano and spices is breaded and fried until crispy. It is the perfect indulgence and goes great with wine or Sangria. Only the Albóndigas (handmade pork meatballs with a unique tomato brandy sauce) rival the Croquetas when it comes to the Tapas Bravas best sellers list.

Sweet Po Tater Tots with Feta-Ranch Dipping Sauce

Courtesy of Dock and Roll Diner

A sweet, savory, tangy labor of love that is worth getting your best cast-iron pan on the job. Pre-prepped tots will last 4 to 5 days covered in the refrigerator.

3 sweet potatoes

kosher salt, to taste

pepper, to taste

frying oil

all-purpose flour, a pinch or two as needed

1–2 eggs as needed, beaten

¼ cup Ken's Home-style Ranch Dressing

¼ cup feta cheese, crumbled

- Heat frying oil to approximately 325°F (no more than 340°F). Cut sweet potatoes into small ½-inch cubes and season gently with kosher salt and pepper.

- When oil is ready, fry pieces of sweet potato in small batches for about 1½ minutes, or until about 75 percent cooked through. Take out of the fryer and season gently with kosher salt and pepper. Let cool for 2 to 3 minutes.

- Place fried sweet potato into a food processor and pulse gently until the pieces have turned into crumbles. Be diligent and watch the pieces process. Do not over pulse them.

- When the potatoes are nicely crumbled, take them out of the blender and place them on the table. Use a rolling pin and a little flour to level out the crumbled potato mixture. You want the mixture to be about an inch high. Make sure not to use too much flour, as it will result in a dry, floury taste at the end.

- Use a small, thumb-sized cookie cutter to cut out individual tots from the leveled potato mixture. Reserve individual tots on a sheet tray dusted with all-purpose flour until ready to fry.

- Dust the finished tots with a little flour, then dip them into the beaten egg, pat off the excess egg and place them back into the flour before dropping them in the fryer. Fry tots for about 3 minutes. When they are ready, remove the tots from the fryer and shake off excess oil. Season gently with kosher salt and pepper.

- While the tots are frying, prepare your dipping sauce by combining about equal parts of the ranch dressing of your choosing and crumbled feta cheese.

WhataQueso with Chips

Courtesy of WhaTaTaco

Queso is one of Austinites' favorite dips. With appetizers like these, who needs a meal?
Yield: 10–15 servings.

1 block Velveeta cheese (16 ounces), cubed

1 block jalapeño cream cheese (8 ounces)

½ cup 2 percent milk

1 tomato, chopped into small cubes

1 onion, chopped into small cubes

1 cilantro, chopped

• Using a Crock-Pot on low heat, slowly melt the Velveeta, adding the jalapeño cream cheese and milk, for about 7 to 10 minutes or until melted, stirring frequently.

• Add the tomato, onions and cilantro into the cheese mixture and stir. If you want a thinner queso, you can add more milk, being sure to stir thoroughly. Keep the queso warm until you serve.

yellow corn tortillas

pinch of sea salt, to taste

Tortilla Chips:

• Cut the tortillas in quarters: 4 wedge-shaped pieces for every tortilla. Add a pinch of sea salt and place them in the oven to toast, just a few minutes on a very high temperature (375°F–400°F). Remove the chips when they are crispy and brownish but not burnt.

WhaTaTaco, Ray Gonzalez

Ray Gonzalez had a restaurant fifteen years prior to opening his food trailer. "Everything started with an idea from my son, and it had a ripple effect," shares Ray. After purchasing the 1972 Airstream trailer, it took him about three months to have everything repurposed, including the final touches to get it ready for business. Lucky number one may have something to do with Ray's success at WhaTaTaco: his grand opening was on 11-11-11 at 11:11 a.m.

Ray will tell you that all of the tacos have their own unique flavor, making it hard to determine a bestseller or pick a personal favorite. However, he makes sure to start his Saturday mornings with a fully loaded barbacoa taco. Originally from Monterrey, Mexico, Ray went to school at Saint Edwards in Austin and loves to call Austin home. His best customers know which salsas to put on which tacos and help new customers pick and choose the different combinations. You can eat inside the Airstream, at a table or on a picnic table in the shade outside.

Wurst Tex Truffle Fries

Courtesy of Wurst Tex

Truffle oil is a contemporary ingredient that is available year-round. Cheaper than truffles themselves, this oil is popular among modern chefs.
Yield: roughly four servings/one potato per person.

4 Russet or Kinnebec potatoes

2 quarts canola frying oil

season salt, to taste

1 tablespoon rosemary, finely chopped

1 tablespoon parsley, finely chopped

2 tablespoons white truffle oil

• Rinse and scrub whole potatoes. Either peel or leave the skins on, according to personal taste. Cut the potatoes into ¼- by ¼-inch-thick sticks. Rinse the cut potatoes in a large bowl with lots of cold running water until water becomes clear. Cover with water by 1 inch and cover with ice. Refrigerate at least 30 minutes or up to 2 days.

• In a 5-quart pot, or in an electric deep fryer, heat oil over medium-low heat until the temperature registers 325°F. You need to have at least 3 inches of space between the top of the oil and the top of the pan, as fries will bubble up when they are added.

• Drain ice water from cut fries and wrap potato pieces in a clean dishcloth or tea towel and thoroughly pat dry. Increase the heat to medium-high and add fries, one handful at a time, to the hot oil. Fry, stirring occasionally, until potatoes are soft and limp and begin to turn a blond color, about 6 to 8 minutes. Using a skimmer or a slotted spoon, carefully remove fries from the oil and set aside to drain on paper towels. Let rest for at least 10 minutes or up to 2 hours.

• When ready to serve the French fries, reheat the oil to 350°F. Transfer the blanched potatoes to the hot oil and fry again, shaking frequently, until golden brown and puffed, about 1 minute. Transfer to paper-lined platter and sprinkle with season salt, rosemary and parsley to taste. Transfer fries to serving dish and drizzle with truffle oil to taste.

Wurst Tex, Sam and Leslie Raver

Without a wealth of culinary expertise, Sam and fiancée Leslie, along with Sam's stepdad, set out for a new chapter of their lives and developed a straightforward sausage concept for their first shot at the trailer food business. Their menu of exotic game sausages, however, is miles from the standard bratwurst experience. From rattlesnake, venison, rabbit, duck and more to regular sausages and extraordinary vegetarian options, the Wurst Tex menu is truly unique.

The Predator and Prey is Sam's personal favorite. It contains rattlesnake, rabbit and pork with jalapeños. Two fun options for vegetarians that look like real sausage links are the '04 Delight, a combination of smoked apples, sage and potatoes, and the Veggiano, which contains eggplant, fennel and garlic.

Bow Wow Chow Salmon Parmesan Dog Treats

Courtesy of Bow Wow Chow

Chef Lara has had several people tell her that their cats love the salmon Parmesan biscuits as much as their dogs do!
Yield: 4 dozen treats.

1 egg

¼ cup vegetable oil

2½ cups flour

½ cup Parmesan cheese

6 ounces canned salmon with liquid

¼ cup powdered milk

¼ cup water

• Preheat oven to 350°F. Scramble egg with oil and add all ingredients to the bowl. Mix thoroughly. Form into dog bite–sized treats and bake for 18 minutes.

Bow Wow Chow

Food trucks aren't just for people. The Bow Wow Chow truck was inspired by a childhood love of the Mystery Machine from *Scooby Doo* and a love for food trucks and dogs. It was as simple as combining these loves when Lara Enzor created Austin's first mobile food truck for dogs.

Dog treats are for every dog and every kind of dog owner. Tough guys will stop and buy ice cream for their pit bulls. Grandparents whip out their cellphones to snap pictures of their dogs eating peanut butter treats. Kids walk up and want to try a bite, and they can! The doggie treats are all natural made with the highest grade of human ingredients (no preservatives or sweeteners). Lara makes an effort to taste every item she sells.

She recalls, "Once at Auditorium Shores' off-leash dog area, a black Labrador raced about fifty yards across the grass straight for the truck. When he reached the truck, he literally stood on his hind legs and put his front paws on the service shelf. I was laughing out loud when his owner showed up two minutes later, empty leash in hand, looking for his dog. Somehow that dog knew that we had treats just for him!"

Sauces

Award-Winning Gypsy Habanero Sauce
Dock and Roll Diner

Carrot Cake Jam
Biscuits and Groovy

Chimichurri Sauce
Conscious Cravings

Cilantro—Pumpkin Seed Pesto
The Fat Cactus

Greenbelt Sauce
Dock and Roll Diner

Lucky J's Jerk Sauce & Dressing
Lucky J's Chicken & Waffles

Rib Glaze & Guacamole
Woodpile BBQ

Sexy Sauce
Cow Bell's

Sour Cream Sriracha Sauce
Cazamance

The Miyagi
The Jalopy

Award-Winning Gypsy Habanero Sauce

Courtesy of Dock and Roll Diner

This sauce won first place in the Austin Chronicle Hot Sauce Festival 2011. It is an extremely spicy sauce with a wonderful citrus disposition that complements the natural orangey flavors from the habanero peppers. It will keep for about two to three weeks in the refrigerator.

25–30 habanero peppers, stemmed

2 gypsy peppers, stemmed

1 Mexibell pepper

1 Cajun bell pepper

1 New Mexico red chile pepper (Note: If only red bell peppers are available, then use 1 large instead of the Mexi, Cajun and New Mexico red chile)

1 Roma tomato

3–4 garlic cloves (peel on)

1 large navel orange, halved

1 lemon, halved

kosher salt and pepper, to taste

oil, to drizzle

water, as needed

• Preheat oven to 425°F. Line ½ sheet tray with foil and lay habanero, gyspy, Mexibell/Cajun bell/New Mexico red chile (or red bell), tomato and garlic on sheet tray with space between each. Drizzle with oil and season with kosher salt and pepper, tossing the ingredients to fully coat with both.

• Roast ingredients in the oven approximately 6 to 8 minutes, turning halfway to not scorch one side. The habanero peppers may finish a couple of minutes before the others due to their size, so be sure to check the oven after 10 to 12 minutes to make sure they are not burning. Take the habaneros out early if needed. The other ingredients should be ready in about 14 to 16 minutes. You will probably be able to smell them in the air when ready.

• After roasting, place ingredients in a covered container to steam for at least 15 minutes and up to 3 days refrigerated.

• When you are ready to make the sauce, remove excess steamed skin from peppers before placing all ingredients in blender with the juice from the orange and half of the lemon, a pinch of salt and pepper. Turn blender on low power and drizzle in oil, then bring it up to medium. When fully combined, check the consistency: sauce should be thick but also smooth and squeezable. If necessary, add a little water to help the blender get it there.

• This is the hard part: taste the sauce. It should, and will, be extremely spicy. But it should have mouthwatering balance. If it is too overpowering without enough of this depth of flavor from the habanero, bell pepper, orange and garlic, then add the juice from the other half of lemon. If the sauce is very spicy but not overpowering with nice flavor but could still seemingly use something, add a pinch of pepper and kosher salt to taste. If you add any ingredients after the taste test, combine again in blender to achieve desired consistency and taste once more. The sauce will be there if the steps were followed, and it will mellow and deepen in flavor as it rests over the next day or two.

Dock and Roll Diner, Lee Krasner, Daniel Dennis and Adam Lewis

Upon finishing culinary school, Lee Krasner had cooked in various kitchens in New York and San Franciscio. When he moved back to his hometown of Austin, he became interested in starting a food trailer concept of his own. "It [the food trailer] provided a lower risk and upfront-cost way of getting to run my own business, to create a menu and concept, to get to be in business for ourselves and do things the way we believe are best," shares Lee.

He took the idea to Daniel Dennis, a friend from Austin who brought with him many years of customer service experience, as well as his experience cooking growing up in a traditional Mexican family. The pair brought Lee's childhood friend Adam Lewis on board to help with business development, and they all began working together as a team to execute the Dock and Roll Diner.

Lee shares more about the '50s Airstream diner: "I bought our 1957 Flying Cloud Airstream Trailer from a great guy named Bruce Ford who collects trailers and lives outside Temple in Mofitt, Texas. We had to do a complete renovation of it and tried to keep the '50s diner theme alive. To help build it out, we had the help of a couple Costa Rican brothers who do really great work here in town."

The Dock and Roll Diner's concept was born out of the idea of serving lobster rolls. The Maine Event is their bestseller. It is a Maine-style lobster roll with claw, knuckle and leg meat chilled and dressed lightly with Old Bay lemon butter and chopped chive for garnish.

Carrot Cake Jam

Courtesy of Biscuits and Groovy

Use this jam to turn a breakfast biscuit into a sweet treat.
Yield: 3.5 pints.

2 cups finely shredded carrots

1 cup finely chopped and pealed pear

1 15-ounce can crushed pineapple (juice packed), undrained

2 tablespoons lemon juice

1 teaspoon ground cinnamon

½ teaspoon ground nutmeg

1 package liquid/gel fruit pectin

4 cups granulated sugar

2 cups packed brown sugar

½ cup flaked coconut

1 teaspoon vanilla

• In a sauce pot, combine carrots, pear, pineapple with the juice, lemon juice, cinnamon and nutmeg. Bring to boil, stirring constantly; reduce heat. Simmer, covered, for 20 minutes, stirring frequently. Remove from the heat. Add pectin.

• Bring mixture to boil, stirring constantly. Add granulated sugar and brown sugar. Return to a full rolling boil and boil for 1 minute, stirring constantly. Remove from heat. Quickly skim off foam with a metal spoon. Stir in coconut and vanilla.

• Pour hot jam into sterilized jars, leaving a ¼-inch headspace. Wipe jar rims, adjust lids.

• Process filled jars in a boiling water bath for 10 minutes. Remove and cool.

Biscuits and Groovy, Jonathan Lach

Jon Lach started Biscuits and Groovy as a vegan trailer with one dish called Biscuits + Groovy. But when his customers saw the sign, many of them were interested in a broader menu. Ultimately, Jon can make any of his dishes with real meats, vegan or vegetarian. "Although I was inspired by Counter Culture and wanted a vegan trailer, it was in my best interest to change it up," shares Jon.

The Biscuits and Groovy trailer serves large, fluffy homemade vegan biscuits topped with a variety of options. Their product names give a nod to musical icons of the past. The Gloria Gaynor, for example, is a dish of three open-face biscuits piled high with gravy, three scrambled eggs, sausage, jalapeños, bacon, cheese, chives and pepper. The Village Biscuits are fully loaded with gravy, veggie sausage, jalapeños, cheese, chives, pepper and Sriracha. Kids get a kick out of the Bee Gees, which are a simple butter and jelly of the day combo on top of Jon's famous biscuits.

Chimichurri Sauce

Courtesy of Conscious Cravings

It's fun to say, easy to make and tastes great!

⅓ cup fresh cilantro

¾ cup fresh parsley

3 cloves garlic, chopped

⅓ cup fresh oregano leaves

¼ cup fresh lemon juice

salt and freshly ground pepper to taste

⅓ cup olive oil

• Combine all ingredients into a blender and blend on low until you reach desired consistency. Refrigerate until ready to use.

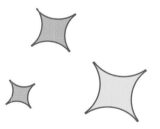

Conscious Cravings, Rishi Dhir

Rishi Dhir left a career in finance and trading to create a fresh start with his food trailer concept. "I wanted to create a fresh, healthy, organic, affordable and tasty fast-food concept that is also scalable," says Rishi. "It took about three months of researching the market for such a niche product, developing the recipes and deciding which equipment to use so that we can provide quick service but still push out a great product. Since I am not much of a cook, my mother and aunt helped me create the recipes that I was envisioning. We spent time critiquing and taste-testing different recipes," he shares.

Conscious Cravings serves healthy foods and caters to specific cuisines: vegetarian, vegan and gluten-free. Many of their ingredients are organic. Almost everything is made from scratch inside the trailers, including all of the sauces and their popular seitan. The Spicy Chickpea Wrap is the most popular item on the menu among the three locations. This wrap contains chickpeas with Indian-style spices, along with lettuce, tomatoes, onions and their chimichurri sauce wrapped in a toasted tortilla.

"My favorite things about the food trailer business are the independence it gives me, providing local jobs and getting to meet so many awesome Austinites when I'm talking with customers," says Rishi.

Cilantro—Pumpkin Seed Pesto

Courtesy of The Fat Cactus

Enjoy on sandwiches, pizzas, pastas or as a marinade.
Yield: about 10 ounces.

2 cups packed fresh cilantro, rinsed and dried (2 bunches)

3 medium garlic cloves

¼ cup unsalted pepitas (pumpkin seeds)

¼ cup cotija or parmesan cheese

1 jalapeño pepper, seeded (or not if you want it spicy) and roughly chopped

juice of 1 lime

¼ cup olive oil

kosher salt and freshly cracked black pepper, to taste

• Place cilantro, garlic, pepitas, cheese, jalapeño and lime juice in food processor. Pulse until well chopped, then scrape down the sides. Run processor and drizzle in olive oil slowly to emulsify. Season with salt and pepper to taste.

Greenbelt Sauce

Courtesy of Dock and Roll Diner

Inspired by the popular hiking, swimming and biking area in Austin, the Greenbelt sauce contains plenty of green ingredients to make your taste buds water.

12–15 large tomatillos, husked and stemmed

2 jalapeños, stemmed, halved and chopped (use 3 if more heat is desired)

1 Hatch chile, stemmed, roasted and chopped

3–4 cloves garlic, roasted

pepper, to taste

kosher salt, to taste

water or chicken or beef stock, to taste

1 large avocado, halved and cored (seed removed)

lime juice, to taste

cilantro, small handful of leaves, stems okay

• Roast tomatillos, jalapeños and Hatch chile on flattop grill with skins on for 4 to 5 minutes per side until charred but not scorched. Or you can roast the same ingredients in oven at 425°F for 10 to 12 minutes. When ready, place them in a covered container to steam the skin for at least 10 minutes or up to 3 days refrigerated, until ready to use.

• Place tomatillos in blender with jalapeños, Hatch chile and garlic with a pinch of pepper and kosher salt and turn blender on low to get started. Then blend tomatillo mixture on medium until combined. If the blender is having a hard time combining, add a little water or stock to bring it together. When tomatillos are fully combined, add avocado pulp, lime and cilantro, but don't add more seasoning until you taste it.

• It will probably need more seasoning; adjust as necessary and blend again. This sauce should have flavor of the acidic tomatillo, creamy avocado and depth of flavor from the jalapeño, Hatch chile, garlic, lime and cilantro.

Lucky J's Jerk Sauce & Dressing

Courtesy of Lucky J's Chicken & Waffles

This sauce is essentially a condiment that can be used on any cooked item or as a marinade. The dressing is for salad or slaw. You'll need to make the jerk sauce in order to make the jerk dressing. Fire is involved.

Jerk Sauce:

2 cups dark spiced rum

½ cup fresh lime juice

½ cup Worcestershire sauce

½ cup apple cider vinegar

½ cup rice vinegar

• Combine liquid ingredients in a pot under medium heat. Add:

3 tablespoons minced fresh ginger

2 tablespoons fresh garlic, minced

1 teaspoon minced and de-seeded fresh habanero pepper

8 tablespoons sugar

1 tablespoon crushed red pepper

1 tablespoon nutmeg

1 tablespoon cinnamon

1 tablespoon dried onion

1 teaspoon ground black pepper

1 teaspoon dried ground thyme

1 teaspoon allspice

1 teaspoon salt

• When the liquid starts to simmer, carefully ignite the mixture to allow the alcohol to burn off (it will flame out of the pot!). Reduce heat and simmer until the liquid has a sauce-like consistency, about 15 minutes.

Jerk Dressing:

1 cup Lucky J's Jerk Sauce

1 cup extra-virgin olive oil

½ cup rice vinegar

juice of one lemon

2 teaspoons fresh minced ginger

½ teaspoon salt

½ teaspoon ground black pepper

• Combine ingredients in a mixing bowl and whisk until the oil mixture is emulsified.

Lucky J's Chicken & Waffles, Jason Umlas

"Chicken for Strength, Waffles for Speed" is the tagline on Jason Umlas's food trailers. Originally from New York, Jason came to Austin by way of Los Angeles. A graduate of Brown University, Jason worked in both the entertainment and Internet industries before leaving a company he founded in order to explore a career in the restaurant business.

Jason's menu is inspired by his many travels, including having lived in Japan and Australia. The Ms. M's Waffle Taco is one of his bestsellers. It is a handheld wrap that includes boneless fried chicken strips with bacon and Swiss, plus a little powdered sugar. The Thai Die is another popular choice that allows customers to indulge in fried chicken, fried banana, peanut butter, honey and Sriracha.

Woodpile BBQ, Levi Smith

With a background in law and after ten years in the healthcare industry, Levi Smith was ready to pursue a new line of work. Newly committed to following their passions, he and his wife serve BBQ on Saturdays out of a food trailer. When he's not barbequing at the trailer, Levi remains an active blogger on the subjects of leadership, technology and productivity. He consults with companies that want to improve their culture or environments and works as a leadership coach with executives and managers who want to get better at leading and serving their teams.

He says, "Barbecue runs deep in my veins. I grew up on a cattle ranch in Driftwood, about twenty miles southwest of Austin, Texas. Back then, if my mom wanted a break from cooking, there was only one option for dine-in or take-out: Salt Lick Bar-B-Que. About once a week for more than twelve years, my family would grab some Salt Lick, and I fell in love with the cuisine and their unique sauce. While attending undergrad at Washington University in St. Louis, my appreciation for barbecue expanded as I savored the regional flavors from Kansas City and Memphis.

For the past fifteen years, I have enjoyed barbecuing for family and friends. I am passionate about gathering people to enjoy delicious food. From small dinner parties to large group events, feeding people is my favorite pastime. I enjoy serving barbecue, homemade ice cream and pies more than anything else.

Brisket is my barbecue bellwether and my favorite item on the menu. We start with exceptional quality, all-natural beef raised on small family farms. I season it with my homemade dry rub and then smoke it over a wood fire for twelve to sixteen hours until it's tender. It's important to me that it's still very moist throughout, has a distinct bark and a thick smoke ring."

Rib Glaze & Guacamole

Courtesy of Woodpile BBQ

With the leftovers of this rib glaze, you can make a mean guac'.

1 red bell pepper

2 tablespoons butter, vegetable oil or virgin olive oil

4 garlic cloves, diced

½ large sweet onion, diced

12 ounces of your favorite beer (ale recommended)

8 ounces of your favorite barbecue sauce (Woodpile BBQ sauce recommended!)

Rib Glaze:

• Blister a red bell pepper in the oven or on the grill until outer skin begins to blacken. Once blackened, carefully remove from oven or grill and peel away outer skin. Chop remaining bell pepper.

• Heat butter (or vegetable or olive oil) in a medium skillet. Place garlic, onion and bell pepper in sizzling skillet and cook until garlic begins to brown and onion caramelizes or becomes translucent.

• Pour 12 ounces of your favorite beer in the skillet. Simmer for 5 to 10 minutes on medium heat. Pour 8 ounces of barbecue sauce into a 1-quart container. Place strainer over 1-quart container and pour in contents of skillet and stir together. When your ribs are ready, pull off the grill and baste with the glaze. Let sit for 15 to 30 minutes before serving.

1–2 avocados

Guacamole:

• Remove skin and pit from avocados and mash to desired texture. Pour garlic, bell pepper and onion from strainer into guacamole. Scrape any bits left over in the skillet into guacamole. Mix together and serve.

Sexy Sauce

Courtesy of Cow Bell's

This BBQ-ranch combo sauce pairs well with sweet potato fries and tater tots.

1 cup buttermilk

1 cup mayonnaise

1 pack ranch mix (yields 32 ounces)

½ cup BBQ sauce (sweet; we like Sweet Baby Ray's BBQ sauce)

½ teaspoon cayenne pepper

• In a medium-sized mixing bowl, add buttermilk first, followed by mayonnaise and ranch mix. Mix well with your whisk of choice. Add BBQ sauce and cayenne and whisk once more until fully combined.

Sour Cream Sriracha Sauce

Courtesy of Cazamance

This sauce goes well with quesadillas, tacos and other popular street foods. Yield: 1 cup.

4 cloves garlic, chopped finely

1–2 tablespoons grape seed oil

pinch of brown sugar

2 sprigs fresh thyme, chopped finely

salt and pepper to taste

1 cup sour cream

1 tablespoon Sriracha or to taste

• In a skillet, caramelize the chopped garlic in grape seed oil with a pinch of brown sugar about 2 to 3 minutes, taking care not to burn. Add thyme, salt and pepper. Let the mixture cool in the refrigerator about an hour until it is really cold. Add sour cream and sriracha, blending evenly by stirring with a spoon.

The Miyagi

Courtesy of The Jalopy

"Having a Filipino-American chef born in Hong Kong lends a unique spin on our Asian-inspired specials. One of the customer favorites is The Miyagi, a miso-based ginger sauce. The fresh, tangy flavor is a great addition on our braised chicken sandwiches. As a recommendation for everyone at home, drizzling the sauce on salads with some daikon or matchstick carrots will make a great snack. Using it as a marinade for fish or chicken will make an entrée for which to die," says Jalopy Jake Miller.

1 cup diced ginger

2 teaspoons mirin (a sweetener traditionally used in Japanese cuisine)

2 cloves garlic

2 tablespoons lemon juice

1½ cups oil (soybean, vegetable or sesame)

3 scallions sliced

½ cup miso

coarsely ground black pepper to taste

• Combine diced ginger, mirin, garlic, lemon juice and oil. At The Jalopy, we typically use soybean oil for this sauce, but you're welcome to use others such as vegetable oil or sesame oil for a warmer, nuttier flavor. Using an immersion blender or food processor, blend until smooth.

• Add scallions, miso and black pepper and blend until combined. The scallions add some nice color and crunch to the sauce, so be careful not to blend too much!

• Give your sauce a taste! Depending on your personal preferences, you may want to add more miso or mirin. The miso is already pretty salty, so be mindful of that when adjusting your recipe. If you think the sauce is too salty, throw some mirin in there to balance it out.

The Jalopy, Nic Patrizi and Jalopy Jake Miller

"We proudly own the largest truck in Austin. It's a Freightliner FL180. We have a sleeper cab with bunk beds for long nights in the kitchen. I found it in a salvage yard in Beaumont, Texas. The previous owner was a hoarder, so we had to clear out a few dumpsters' worth of wild stuff. A few welding lessons later, and now I have a kitchen," shares Chef Nic Patrizi.

Nic was born in Texas and grew up in Switzerland; Jake, also born in Texas, came of age in Alaska. Chef Sarah, born in Hong Kong and raised in the Philippines, finally found Texas and calls Austin her home. Through their many travels and experiences with cuisine from around the world, the team at The Jalopy has incorporated some of their favorite flavors and ingredients into a multicultural menu. They have delicious braised chicken and seven housemade sauces and are one of the only trailers in Austin baking homemade bread.

"I grew up around food in my grandparents' Italian restaurant and lived abroad, giving me a unique view of the culinary world. Eating has always been a passion, and after graduating from McCombs Business School at the University of Texas, I knew I wanted to own a restaurant," says founding partner Nic Patrizi. "After eating here multiple times a day for two years, I've concluded my favorite is the Gad Thai. Named after my friend Ryan Gad and inspired by pad thai, it is a coconut-based peanut sauce served with our amazing red wine vinaigrette pickled onions," shares chef Nic.

"Similar to Nic, I've been eating here for two years, and it's made me a dog for the specials. My particular favorite is The Miyagi. It's a delicious miso-based ginger sauce that Sarah makes up for us. Often we serve it with our house pickled radishes, giving me something new," says Nic's partner in crime, Jalopy Jake. Another Jalopy staff favorite is the Suite 709. "It's our chicken sandwich with a Mexican version of a traditional pesto, made with cilantro and tomatillos rather than basil. The sauce is so versatile I end up putting it on everything I eat: breakfast tacos, salads, you name it," shares Sarah.

You can't miss the big rig serving radical sandwiches downtown in a parking lot close to no other trailer. Their typical customers are a range of Austinites who live and work downtown. "I get pretty stoked when former Speaker of the House Gib Lewis comes by. He tips in two-dollar bills," shares Jalopy Jake.

San Marcos: A Day Trip to the Trailers

ollege towns are popular sites for trailer food parks, and San Marcos is no exception to the rule. Just half an hour down the road from Austin, the home of the Texas State Bobcats offers a variety of food truck concepts.

Root Beer Float (Hold the Root)
How Sweet It Is

Vanilla Bean Gluten-Free Scones
Lovebaked

Pick Me Up Cupcake
Lovebaked

The Caboose, Bruce Bryson

Jalapeño Popper Burger
The Patty Wagon

Black Bean Veggie Burger
The Patty Wagon

Fried Oreos
The Patty Wagon

Ponzu Sauce
The Big Kahuna

Loco Moco
The Big Kahuna

Root Beer Float (Hold the Root)

Courtesy of How Sweet It Is

The Hitch is a BYOB trailer lot. Its owners noticed that many of their customers bring higher-quality beers to enjoy with their food. They serve gelato in their trailer and floats (they like to say they'll make just about anything into a float), and this got their wheels turning. They did a little research and have come up with some good beer/gelato pairings.

2 scoops Sea Salt Caramel Gelato

6–8 ounces of your favorite banana bread–flavored beer

caramel syrup

• Place two scoops of our Sea Salt Caramel Gelato into a 20-ounce cup (a frosty mug would be good too, we just don't have them at the trailer). Slowly pour beer over the gelato (*watch out! If you pour too fast, there could be a sticky mess). Drizzle the caramel syrup on top.

How Sweet It Is, Monica Coggin and Peggy Honaker

The mother-and-daughter team of Peggy Honaker and Monica Coggin decided they wanted to work together. Meeting in Wimberley, Monica moved from Austin and Peggy moved from west Texas to start their family business. "We explored several menu options but chose cupcakes because we already had some delicious recipes. We started with six flavors and sold close to two thousand cupcakes in our first full month of being open. That's all it took: we were hooked! Within three months of opening, we bought out the local special-order bakery and expanded our line to include custom cakes and wedding cakes," the team shares.

The Red Velvet and Chocolate Truffle compete for the spot as most popular cupcake, but the Spiced Pumpkin exceeds all sales goals when the fall rolls in. Many of the recipes were inspired by Peggy's mom (Monica's grandmother), Lina, who was from Munich, Germany.

Vanilla Bean Gluten-Free Scones

Courtesy of Lovebaked

A gluten-free Lovebaked treat.

Scones:

¾ cups sour cream

1 egg

seeds from a vanilla bean pod or 1 teaspoon vanilla bean paste

2 cups gluten free flour

⅓ cup sugar

1 tablesppon baking powder (make sure it's GF)

¼ teaspoon baking soda

½ teaspoon salt

¼ teaspoon xantham gum

6 tablespoons cold unsalted butter, cubed

Vanilla Bean Glaze:

1 cup powdered sugar

¼ teaspoon vanilla bean paste

1–2 tablespoons milk

• Whisk all ingredients together until smooth.

• Making the scones: Preheat oven to 425°F. Whisk together sour cream, egg and vanilla bean in a small bowl; set aside.

• In a food processor, pulse flour, sugar, baking powder, baking soda, salt and xantham gum together. Add the cubed butter and pulse until a coarse meal forms. Pulse in the wet ingredients until just combined.

• Scoop batter onto a parchment-lined cookie sheet using an ice cream scoop. Bake for 10 to 12 minutes, or until a toothpick inserted into the middle of one comes out clean.

• Drizzle glaze over the top of scones and enjoy!

Lovebaked, India Moore and Celena McGuill

India Moore was baking so many cakes, cookies and cupcakes for friends that she eventually rented space at a commercial kitchen and began selling her products to coffee shops in New Braunfels and San Antonio. With the help of her family, she turned a shiny silver trailer into a working kitchen as a spot to sell her Lovebaked desserts and gourmet espresso in 2010. "We worked on the trailer every weekend as a family. It was a lot of hard work, but worth it," shares India about the 1966 Airstream she originally bought for $1,500. "We got it in Austin and outfitted the entire thing ourselves. We gutted the entire thing down to the frame, reinforced the frame by welding new steel members, did the electrical, plumbing, welding of tables, sheetmetal work all ourselves. We ordered all of the equipment to fit. The only thing we didn't do ourselves was make the ventahood."

Next door to India and her family lived their good friends the McGuills. Celena McGuill had been in the marketing industry for nearly fifteen years before she was laid off, and although it was in her DNA, she had never considered a career in baking. As fate would allow, Celena joined India in the gourmet dessert business as a partner in 2011. Celena shares, "My grandfather owned a successful bakery for many years before he passed away, and my mom had a cake/dessert business for many years. She still bakes out of her home for friends and family. I can remember going to my grandfather's bakery as a little girl and getting excited when I saw the rows and rows of sweet bread, cookies, cupcakes and other sweet treats in the display cases. While in high school, by default, I was my mom's unpaid help. I remember having to go with her to weddings on Saturday nights to help serve the cake and would set aside an oversized piece for myself before serving it to everyone else to make sure I got one before it ran out. It was my favorite part of the evening! That was always my favorite part of any wedding, birthday or event. I considered myself a cake connoisseur, as I have eaten many a cake over the years! Before now, I never thought I would have had a career in cake. Now I know cake has always been my destiny!"

It is hard to resist sitting at a pink table in front of a shiny Airstream trailer serving delicious, fresh confections. Among their bestsellers is the Senorita Cupcake, which is a chocolate cake infused with cinnamon and topped with cinnamon cream cheese frosting. Others say the Peanut Butter Blackout is the way to go. It is chocolate cake filled with a peanut butter cream filling and frosted with chocolate buttercream frosting, plus a mini Reese's plunked on top. Still others claim the Strawberry Fields is Lovebaked's best cupcake. Fresh strawberry puree is baked into the cake and mixed in the buttercream frosting, and the cupcake is topped with a fresh strawberry drizzle.

Pick Me Up Cupcake

Courtesy of Lovebaked

Lovebaked gets 15 cupcakes from this recipe, but their liners are slightly larger than your standard-size cupcake. For standard-size cupcakes, you should get around 2 dozen.

Cupcakes:

1 cup unsalted butter

½ cup Dutch process cocoa powder

4 ounces fresh-brewed Cuvee Coffee Espresso (Dead Fingers Blend)

¼ cup water

2 cups granulated sugar

½ cup buttermilk

1 tablespoon pure Mexican vanilla

1 teaspoon orange extract

2 large eggs

2 cups all-purpose flour

1 teaspoon baking soda

¼ teaspoon salt

Pick Me Up Frosting:

1 tablespoon fresh-brewed Cuvee Coffee espresso (Dead Fingers Blend)

1 tablespoon milk

1 cup unsalted butter, softened to room temperature

¼ cup cocoa powder, sifted

4 cups sifted powdered sugar

1 teaspoon pure Mexican vanilla

1 teaspoon orange extract

To Make the Frosting:

• Mix espresso and milk together; set aside. Using the wire whisk attachment of your stand mixer, whip the butter on medium-high speed for 3 minutes, stopping to scrape the bowl once or twice.

• Reduce the speed to low and gradually add the cocoa powder and powdered sugar. Once all the cocoa and powdered sugar is incorporated, add the extracts and milk/espresso mixture. Whip at medium-high speed until light and fluffy, about 2 minutes, scraping the bowl as needed.

To Make the Cupcakes:

• Preheat oven to 350°F and line standard cupcake pan with paper liners.

• Melt butter in a large heavy saucepan over moderately low heat, then whisk in cocoa. Add espresso and water and whisk until smooth. Remove from heat. Whisk in separately sugar, buttermilk, extracts and eggs.

• Sift together flour, baking soda and salt into a bowl. Whisk into wet mixture until combined—don't over mix!

• Fill cupcake papers to about ⅔ full. Bake for 20 minutes or until a toothpick comes out with a few moist crumbs.

• Cool completely, frost and devour!

The Caboose, Bruce Bryson

Bruce Bryson appropriately fell in love with the idea of food vending after visiting the state fair. It was to be expected, coming from a family who loves to cook and share. His grandfather owned a restaurant during the Depression, and following in his footsteps, Bruce opened The Caboose food trailer to cook quality seafood for people in San Marcos. "Once our minds were made up, it took about six months to implement," shares Bruce.

The crab balls (made with 100 percent lump crab) are his bestseller, followed closely by shrimp, hand-battered catfish and calamari top rings. Bruce's personal favorite is the Shrimp Po'Boy, a large hoagie bun stuffed with lettuce, pickles and shrimp smothered in his special spicy sauce. The Caboose also offers a spicy crawfish chowder during cooler months that is made from scratch. The chowder is so good that they always sell out by 2:00 p.m. when they make it.

Some of Bruce's best customers drive several miles to get a taste of The Caboose. Bruce shares, "Once, a pastor from Luling had a guest from out of town. He and his family loved our food so much they brought the guest to eat with us. Doesn't sound so incredible if I stop there, but there was a raging thunderstorm going on. The pastor and friend loaded up the car and drove all the way from Luling in the storm only to order and eat under an umbrella while it rained here too."

Jalapeño Popper Burger

Courtesy of The Patty Wagon

Treat your grilling guests to cream cheese, bacon and jalapeños sealed in a double-decker burger made with jalapeño mayo and a house seasoning.

½ ounce fresh chopped jalapeños

1 ounce cream cheese

2 strips cooked smoked bacon

2 (3-ounce) fresh hamburger patties

house seasoning

buns

Jalapeño Mayo (to taste)

lettuce

tomatoes

pickles

onions

• Sauté jalapeños until al dente, approximately 2 to 3 minutes on medium-low heat. Place cooked jalapeños, cream cheese and bacon between the 2 patties. Seal by pressing around the meat edges.

• Season patty on both sides with house seasoning to taste; cook to desired wellness.

• Toast buns and top burger with other ingredients.

Jalapeño Mayo: (yield: 2 cups)

3 tablespoons fresh pickled jalapeños (chopped)

2 cups mayo

salt, pepper and garlic to taste.

Pickled Jalapeños:

• Add 10 sliced jalapeños in a glass jar; pour pickle juice to cover. Let sit for 3 to 5 days.

House Seasoning: (yield: 1½ cups)

1 cup Season-All

¼ cup powder garlic

¼ cup black pepper

Black Bean Veggie Burger

Courtesy of The Patty Wagon

This is the owner's favorite thing on his menu.

1 (15-ounce) can black beans, rinsed and drained

1 small box sweet cornmeal

1 package Mexican cornmeal

¼ cup fine diced red onion

¼ cup salsa (freshly made, see recipe below)

1 teaspoon pepper

½ teaspoon salt

2 teaspoons fresh minced garlic

olive oil

Black Bean Corn Relish(freshly made, see recipe below)

• Pour black beans into large bowl, mash and add other ingredients except oil and relish. Mix well and make into 4-ounce patties.

• Add olive oil into cast-iron skillet. Press patty down and cook until brown on both sides, about 3 to 4 minutes to cook through.

Black Bean Corn Relish:

1 (15-ounce) can black beans, rinsed and drained

1 (15-ounce) can sweet corn, drained

1 medium avocado, diced

1 small jar of pimentos

½ cup Italian dressing

salt and pepper to taste

• Add all ingredients in large bowl. Mix well and refrigerate 30 minutes prior to use.

Salsa:

2 Roma tomatoes

1 celery stalk

¼ red onion

1 small jalapeño, no seeds

2 tablespoons cilantro

1 tablespoon garlic, minced

½ teaspoon salt and pepper

• Combine all ingredients in blender and blend well.

Fried Oreos

Courtesy of The Patty Wagon

You've seen 'em at the fair. Now you can make 'em at home.

6 Oreos (frozen)

vegetable oil (to deep fry) 350 degrees

powdered sugar, to garnish

chocolate syrup, to garnish

cherries, to garnish

Batter:

2 eggs

1½ cups whole milk

2 cups all-purpose flour

4 teaspoons baking powder

¼ teaspoon salt

• Place Oreos in freezer until frozen (2 hours) prior to dipping into batter.

Preparing the Batter:

• In a small bowl, beat eggs and milk together. In a separate bowl, add dry ingredients (flour, baking powder and salt); mix well. Add wet ingredients to dry ingredients and whisk well (do not over mix).

• Dip Oreos into batter and drop into hot oil (enough to submerge if not using a deep fryer). Brown, tap to flip and brown other side. Place fried Oreos on plate in a circle and dust powdered sugar over Oreos. Place a large dollop of fresh whipped cream in the center of the circle of Oreos; drizzle chocolate syrup over all to taste and top with cherry.

Fresh Whipped Cream:

1 cup heavy whipping cream

4 teaspoons powdered sugar

1 teaspoon Mexican vanilla

Making the Fresh Whipped Cream:

• In large mixing bowl, add whipping cream, powdered sugar and Mexican vanilla. Whip until stiff peaks are formed.

The Patty Wagon, Fred Varela

"My wife and I purchased this trailer to take our son camping; we traveled to various parks around Texas, and when my son lost interest in camping, it sat in the backyard for years until I decided to rip everything out of it and repurpose it to create The Patty Wagon," says Fred.

Born in Chicago, Fred Varela moved to California and then ultimately to Texas when he was a teen. He is now living in Kyle and lived in San Marcos for twenty years prior to that. "I've been in the food service business for thirty-five years. I have worked as a line cook at a truck stop, ran a restaurant in a five-star hotel and managed food service operations at Texas State University—San Marcos. I stopped at a food trailer in San Antonio and remember thinking, 'I'm going to open one of these up' while I was eating," shares Fred. After his son said, "It's hard to find a good, homemade, tasty burger," it took Fred about six months from start to finish to get The Patty Wagon open.

While the bacon cheeseburger may be his bestseller, Fred's favorite item on the menu is his Black Bean Veggie Burger. He starts with four ounces of black beans and adds freshly made salsa, two types of cornmeal and seasonings. The burger is topped with lettuce, tomatoes, onions, pickles and freshly made corn black bean relish and your choice of any of the five freshly made mayonnaises he makes.

The Patty Wagon has a loyal following, including one fellow who will call in his order while he's in the parking lot, walk up to the window (about five minutes) and ask if it's done yet. Every Friday like clockwork.

Ponzu Sauce

Courtesy of The Big Kahuna

Use this sauce as a marinade or grilling aide.

• Prepare this sauce by using 80 percent soy sauce and 20 percent freshly squeezed citrus juice from assorted fruits.

Loco Moco

Courtesy of The Big Kahuna

This is a traditional Hawaiian-style breakfast.

• Take a grilled ⅓-pound hamburger patty and add brown gravy plus a sunny side up egg on top. Serve with white rice.

The Big Kahuna, Mark and Lori Jakobsen

"We serve authentic Hawaiian food, which are family recipes from Maui. We're the only known authentic Hawaiian food between San Antonio and Kileen. We've never had an unsatisfied customer, and we strive for excellence in every bite," say Mark and Lori Jakobsen.

You might not expect a top-notch chef with a gourmet background to be serving Hawaiian food out of a food truck in San Marcos, Texas, but that is exactly what Chef Mark Jakobsen and his wife, Lori, are doing. Mark's culinary background is impressive; he has hosted Clinton's economic summit, represented the National Bison Association at the James Beard Foundation in Manhattan, been a personal chef for a multibillionaire media mogul, catered for Willy Nelson during South by Southwest in Austin and collaborated with other chefs to prepare a dinner honoring Julia Child.

"My stepfather was a chef from Copenhagen, Denmark. My culinary experience started at age nine in Si's Charcoal Broiler, a restaurant that my family owned in Berkeley, California. My family owned five restaurants in Maui, Hawaii. From seafood to sushi to steaks, my family's restaurants served it all," says Mark.

At the trailer, Mark's favorite item on their menu is the Poki, a Hawaiian-style ceviche. Lori loves the Hawaiian-style fish tacos with papaya salsa. Their fans say the Big Kahuna Burger is the best burger they've ever had. In fact, a Texas State student who had been on vacation came all the way from Houston. He told Mark that for the three-hour drive, all he could think about was a Big Kahuna burger, which was his first stop when he arrived in San Marcos, even before unloading his car. The Big Kahuna is indeed a special burger. It is a ⅓-pound fresh, handmade hamburger patty topped with Kahlua pork on a Hawiian sweet bread and served with Kilawea sauce.

Sides

Achiote Mexican Rice
Bufalo Bob's Chalupa Wagon

Hoppin' John
Bufalo Bob's Chalupa Wagon

Bacon Fried Rice with Fried Egg
(Bacon Silog)
Be More Pacific

Borscht Belt Potato Salad
Schmaltz

Goat Cheese Hush Puppies
Kiss My Grits

Jicama Slaw
The Gypsy Kit

Jalapeño Mac 'n' Cheese
SoCo to Go

Lucky J's Jamaican Citrus Slaw
Lucky J's Chicken & Waffles

Momma's Coleslaw
Kiss My Grits

Moroccan Potato Salad
The Flying Carpet

Schmaltz Pickled Okra
Schmaltz

Pistachio Watermelon Salad with Jalapeño
Orange Balsamic Vinaigrette
Kebabalicious

Spring Medley Spinach Salad
Colibri Cuisine

Street Corn
Torchy's Tacos

Achiote Mexican Rice

Courtesy of Bufalo Bob's Chalupa Wagon

An excellent side dish to enchiladas or tamales, Achiote Mexican Rice is full of Yucatan flavor. In this dish, Bufalo Bob likes to mix white and brown rice for a more complete carbohydrate than just white rice.

3 tablespoons olive oil

⅔ cup white rice

⅓ cup brown rice

½ onion, chopped

2 cloves garlic, minced

2¾ cups chicken broth

1 tablespoon Achiote paste

1 poblano pepper, deveined, seeded and diced

1 lime, juice only

pinch of salt

2 tablespoons cilantro, finely chopped

• Put oil into a large skillet and heat to medium-high. Add both rices and cook for about 1 to 2 minutes. Add onions and garlic. Continue cooking until rice starts to turn brown, about 5 to 7 minutes.

• Now add the chicken broth, Achiote paste, poblano pepper, lime juice and salt. Bring mixture to a boil, reduce heat and allow to simmer for 25 to 30 minutes until rice is soft.

• Turn off the heat. Add cilantro, mix and let stand for 5 minutes.

Hoppin' John

Courtesy of Bufalo Bob's Chalupa Wagon

Hoppin' John is a southern dish that is based on black-eyed peas. Many folks eat these on New Year's Day for good luck.

1 cup black-eyed peas, soaked overnight

7 cups water

¾ cup onion, chopped

2 strips bacon, cut into small pieces

3 tablespoons molasses

⅔ cup white rice

⅓ cup brown rice, uncooked

1 teaspoon garlic, minced

½ teaspoon black pepper

• Soak peas in water overnight, rinse and drain. In a pot, bring water to a boil. Add black-eyed peas, onion, bacon and molasses. Reduce heat and boil for about 2 hours or until water content is about half. Add rice, garlic and pepper and cook for another 20 to 30 minutes or until remaining liquid is completely absorbed. Salt to taste before serving.

Bacon Fried Rice with Fried Egg (Bacon Silog)

Courtesy of Be More Pacific

Breakfast meets rice. Mark Pascual says, "The Bacon-Silog or Bacon Fried Rice with Fried Egg is our bestseller and my personal favorite. Silog is a slang term made up of two words: sinangag, *which is garlic fried rice with onions, and* itlog, *which is egg. This dish takes me back to my nights in the Philippines after drinking where we were summoned by the fried garlic of a silog stand. So satisfying, it made you smile with your eyes closed. Our version has crispy bacon, a runny egg and I like to add the tangy spicy sweet of the plantain ketchup. When I'm feeling frisky, I'll add the spicy curry coconut, and that takes it to the next level with a bit of creamyness from the coconut, extra warmth from the curry and the bite of freshness from the lime."*

6–8 strips raw bacon, cut into ¾-inch squares

6 eggs

part of a white onion, diced (about 3 ounces)

1–2 cloves garlic, minced (about 1.5 ounces)

6 cups white rice, cooked

1.5 ounces salt

3 teaspoons garlic powder

• Preferably using a wok, render bacon down by cooking on low-medium heat for 5 to 10 minutes until crisp. Set aside.

• Take 3 of the eggs and scramble. Using a separate pan, cook the scrambled eggs on medium heat for 1 to 2 minutes until done and set aside.

• Using the same wok the bacon was cooked in, sauté the diced onions and minced garlic. Add the white rice and continue to mix over medium-high heat until the rice reaches an almost crispy state. Add the salt and garlic powder to taste and mix thoroughly. Place rice mixture in a serving bowl and fry the rest of the eggs and place on top of the rice.

Be More Pacific, Mark Pascual and Partners Goo Cuchapin and Cristina Luna

Mark says, "The idea of opening a Filipino restaurant always came up when I would crave Adobo or Lumpia, but with all the barriers to entry and the start-up capital needed, opening a Filipino restaurant was always put on the back burner. I always promoted Filipino cuisine the best I could—parties, office potlucks, etc. I knew our food was good and I wanted to tell the world, but no one was listening. Then food trucks entered Austin's culinary dialogue, and with eyebrows raised, we decided this would be our voice for what we had to say."

Inspired by his parents, who loved to cook, Mark grew up eating mismatched dinners like adobo pork with mac and cheese or Pandesal (Filipino bread) with peanut butter and jelly. His dad cooked everything from adobo to gumbo, while his mom made mostly traditional Filipino cuisine. This is why there are fusion items on the Be More Pacific truck. "This is who we are, second-generation Filipino/Americans with a wide palate but don't know how to speak Tagalog as much as we should," says Mark.

If you visit the truck, you may run into Victor, one of their best customers and namesake for a popular dish. The Victor has bacon fried rice with a spicy curry coconut lime upgrade and three eggs. Victor has been known to bring people, sometimes by the arm, up to the truck to give Be More Pacific a shot, guaranteeing they will like it or he will pay for their meal. "Our best customers have the biggest mouths," Mark shares.

Borscht Belt Potato Salad

Courtesy of Schmaltz

Borscht is a popular Eastern European dish made of beets. This potato salad incorporates authentic flavors of Europe into an all-American side dish.

5 pounds red potatoes

about 1½ pounds pickled beets

¼ cup balsamic vinegar

⅓ cup olive oil

¼ cup pickled beet juice

salt and pepper

4 tablespoons fresh chopped dill

1 cup fresh chopped parsley

• Boil whole potatoes in salted water for about 15 to 20 minutes until very tender. Let potatoes cool and then chop into bite-sized chunks. Put potatoes in a big bowl.

• Chop pickled beets the same size as the potatoes or smaller. Add beets to the bowl with the potatoes. Add balsamic vinegar, olive oil and beet juice. Add salt and pepper to taste, along with chopped herbs. Lightly combine the mixture by folding with a large spoon and chill until cooled. Serve slightly chilled.

Schmaltz, Julia Hungerford

"I am very interested in art and literature and try to reflect that in my own business. I name sandwiches after Jewish artists and writers. I do this to perpetuate education. There is history behind the sandwiches. Food is an undeniable expression of culture and tradition and can bring back memories in a way nothing else can. Proust's madeleines are really a perfect example of the way that food shapes our memories and memories shape our ideas of food," says Julia.

Between growing up a vegetarian in Knoxville, Tennessee, and opening her own food trailer in Austin, Texas, Julia Hungerford wore many hats: conducting archaeological surveys, doing summons delivery, teaching art to teenagers and cooking for children at a rec center. In the mountains of northeastern California, she worked for a bakery that sold boiled eggs from the owners' chickens and made bread with locally grown wheat.

When Julia met Sue from Counter Culture (an Austin trailer turned brick-and-mortar restaurant), it resonated with her that Sue was doing this business all on her own. She bought Sue's old trailer, gave it a paint job and opened her doors for business. Entrepreneurialism runs in her family, Julia explains: "My family is full of entrepreneurs. When my grandparents and their brothers and sisters came to America, they dreamed big and started small. My grandparents started out repairing watches in the back of a friends' laundromat in Chicago and ended up running a jewelry store in Nashville. Their store was located in Belle Meade Plaza for about twenty-five years. In the same shopping center, their friends ran Schwartz's Deli. They had giant pickles they made and kept in barrels. I always got a pickle when I was in town. When I was losing teeth as a kid, I think I lost at least two on those pickles. My grandmother is an amazing cook and makes the best cheesecake in the world. She also makes amazing soup and has an eye for fruit at the market. Her brother, my uncle Bernie, ran a lunch truck in San Francisco for a while. She tells me he is watching over me."

The falafel is Julia's favorite. After all, she worked hard to perfect it using fresh herbs and spices and choosing to lightly pan fry it in minimal oil. The Harvey P Seitan "Pastrami" Reuben is by far her bestseller. "I named the sandwich after the comic book writer Harvey Pekar. I make the seitan from scratch, spice it with black pepper and slice it super thin on a deli slicer. I grill marble rye, melt a slice of Swiss if you'd like (or not to make it entirely vegan), pile on the "pastrami," top it with fresh shredded cabbage and then smother it with my own vegan Chipotle Russian dressing. It has a nice smokey sweet flavor that is slightly addictive," explains Julia.

She is inspired by chef Kenny Shopsin, the owner of Shopsin's in New York, because of his large menu and his soups, which are made to order. Not to mention he is the star of *I Like Killing Flies*, a documentary on his restaurant.

M.F.K. Fisher, the essayist, is a huge inspiration to her as well. "She includes recipes, memories, history, science and epicurean concepts in her writing and does it in such a charming way. Her book *Consider the Oyster* begins with the line, 'An oyster leads a dreadful but exciting life,'" shares Julia.

Julia's grandmother Sally Wolkoff is another source of great inspiration both as a businesswoman and a cook. "She makes cheesecakes for her friends and colleagues as gifts, and it really is one of the most special treats in the world. It is made with a sugar cookie crust and has just the right amount of lemon zest. No chocolate, no fruit on top, no graham cracker—those do not make a cheesecake in my book," says Julia.

"The concept of Schmaltz is close to my heart and a little nostalgic. It is also simple yet flexible in a sense that I am not creatively blocked in. For example, I have a reuben, but it is not your traditional East Coast reuben. It's vegetarian and has hints of Mexican cooking. However, it is, of course, on rye!"

Goat Cheese Hush Puppies

Courtesy of Kiss My Grits

"Hush puppies are as reminiscent of my childhood as strawberry Kool-Aid mixed with milk (I ate some weird things) and my Incredible Hulk Big Wheel. They remind me of summer days spent with grandparents and parents on the shores of some lake, catching catfish and bream, and summer nights frying up the day's catch in the driveway. Sadly, most restaurants these days forego making these from scratch in lieu of precooked, frozen balls. As an adult, when I make these for friends, I prefer a slightly more sophisticated version," says Christopher Crowley.

1½ sticks butter

3 cups cornmeal

2 cups all-purpose flour

1 teaspoon baking powder

1 tablespoon baking soda

1 tablespoon coriander

2 tablespoons cumin

2 tablespoons salt

2 teaspoons white pepper

3 eggs

1 pint buttermilk

2¾ cups corn, reserve ¾ cup

1 cup green chile

4 tablespoons cilantro, minced

2 cups goat cheese

• In a medium sauce pan, brown butter over low heat and set aside.

• In a mixing bowl, mix together all dry ingredients.

• In a separate mixing bowl, whisk eggs until smooth. Add buttermilk and brown butter.

• Slowly incorporate wet mix into dry mix.

• In a food processor fitted with a blade attachment, puree first measure of corn. Add to batter.

• In a food processor fitted with a blade attachment, puree green chilies. Add to batter.

• Add second measure of corn to batter whole. Add cilantro.

• Crumble goat cheese and fold into batter.

• Using a one-ounce portion scoop, scoop out batter and drop into a preheated 350°F fryer. Fry in small batches until hush puppies are golden brown and cooked through. Drain on a paper towel and serve immediately.

Jicama Slaw

Courtesy of The Gypsy Kit

Serve on tacos, grilled flank steak, chicken, fish or as a side salad.

1 large jicama, peeled and sliced thin into matchsticks

1 (12-ounce) bag of matchstick carrots

1¼ bunch of cilantro, chopped

juice of two limes

4 scallions, sliced

1 jalapeño, minced

½ teaspoon kosher salt

● Combine all ingredients and season with kosher salt to taste. Let sit in refrigerator overnight to incorporate flavors.

SoCo to Go, Sam Rhodes

Sam Rhodes got the idea to start a lunch delivery business from all the times she spent working through lunch as a controller in the property management industry. She hungered for some new delivery options. Thus, her trailer concept started as a lunch delivery business serving downtown Austin. Delivery is free, and all three of her delivery drivers are in the same band and great friends. SoCo to Go offers dine-in options at the trailer too.

"Both my mother and grandmother have been cooking all of my life and serve as my inspiration for the types of foods I lean toward, mostly southern comfort foods," says Sam. She makes everything from scratch daily, and all of her fried items are hand breaded and fried to order.

Her trailer, "Mae Mae," is homemade too. In her previous life, Mae Mae was used as a dual taco/snow cone trailer. After a paint job, new appliances and a little bit of love, Sam transformed the trailer and had it in business just a week after she purchased it.

Chicken Strips are Sam's favorite item on the menu, served with cream gravy, garlic ranch, barbeque sauce or ketchup for dipping. Her Chicken-Fried Chicken and Ultimate Fish Tacos are two of her bestsellers.

Jalapeño Mac 'n' Cheese

Courtesy of SoCo to Go

A spicier rendition of a classic side dish that utilizes Tony's and Goldfish. Yield: four 3-ounce servings.

12 ounces elbow macaroni noodles

1 teaspoon salt

8 ounces cream cheese

3¼ cups heavy cream

¼ cup jalapeño juice (from pickled jalapeños)

2 cups grated mild cheddar cheese

½ cup chopped pickled jalapeños (mild to medium)

1 tablespoon Tony Cachere's Creole seasoning

1 cup crushed Goldfish crackers

• Boil macaroni until al dente in salted water, approximately 10 minutes. Drain and set aside.

• Heat cream cheese in pot over medium-low heat until melted. Increase heat to medium, add heavy cream and whisk until blended.

• Add jalapeño juice and whisk until blended. Mix in grated cheddar cheese and stir until completely melted.

• Mix in chopped jalapeños and Tony Cachere's seasoning. Whisk until all ingredients are incorporated.

• Add cooked noodles to cheese sauce and stir until well blended.

• Spray half-size hotel pan with nonstick spray. Add noodle/sauce mixture to pan. Top with crushed Goldfish crackers. Let the completed dish sit for at least 10 minutes for the sauce to thicken. Serve as a side with your favorite home-cooked meal.

Lucky J's Jamaican Citrus Slaw

Courtesy of Lucky J's Chicken & Waffles

This colorful dish is rich with island flavors.

2 cups julienned napa cabbage

1 cup julienned red cabbage

1 cup julienned jicama

⅓ cup chopped cilantro

1 teaspoon minced habanero pepper

¾ cup Lucky J's Jerk Dressing (see page 58)

• Toss all the vegetables thoroughly in a large bowl while adding the dressing to your desired consistency, about ¾ of a cup.

Momma's Coleslaw

Courtesy of Kiss My Grits

"This is one of the recipes that I experimented with all through culinary school, before I realized that my mother had already discovered the perfect blend of creamy and tangy styles of coleslaw. I love many different kinds of coleslaw, but if I had a dollar for every person who told me they hated coleslaw before trying this recipe, I would already have a fleet of food trucks. The only alteration I've made to her original recipe is substituting my recipe, Black Pepper Mayonnaise, for the store-bought Blue Plate mayonnaise my mom swears by," says Christopher Crowley.
Yield: 3 quarts.

1 head green cabbage, quartered, cored and julienned

1 yellow onion, julienned

2 Roma tomatoes, seeded and julienned

1 carrot, julienned

1 bunch green onion, sliced thinly on the bias

2 tablespoons salt

½ cup mayonnaise

4 tablespooons apple cider vinegar

1 tablespoon black pepper

• Toss all vegetables in a bowl with the salt. Allow to sit for ten minutes. Mix mayonnaise, vinegar and pepper separately to create a black pepper mayonnaise. Combine dressing with vegetables and refrigerate overnight or until chilled. Serve cold.

Moroccan Potato Salad

Courtesy of The Flying Carpet

This traditional salad is creamy from the olive oil and tangy from the vinegar. It is part of the "lucky seven" salads of Morocco. Traditional homes will have a seven-salad medley as a first course or alongside the main course. The lucky seven are beets, potatoes, green pepper, cucumber, carrots, tomatoes and then rice salad in the middle of the presentation. The number seven is significant in the Moroccan culture: weddings take seven days, there are seven vegetables in the iconic Moroccan couscous dish, the country can be divided into seven major regions and so on.

2 pounds (10–15) small red potatoes

½ small white onion, finely chopped

1 teaspoon cumin

sea salt and black pepper

3–4 tablespoons olive oil

¼ bunch cilantro

3 tablespoons white vinegar

• Boil potatoes until cooked through, approximately 15 to 20 minutes. Cut into big bite-sized chunks. While the potatoes are still warm, add onions, spices, oil, cilantro and vinegar. Mix well and taste. Add more oil and vinegar as needed.

Schmaltz Pickled Okra

Courtesy of Schmaltz

These pickles are ready to eat the next day but especially delightful after one week.
Yield: 1 quart.

3 cups distilled water

1 cup white vinegar

¼ cup kosher salt (Diamond)

enough fresh okra to fill a quart jar completely

3 cloves garlic, whole

3 dried hot peppers

2 sprigs fresh dill

• Heat the water, vinegar and salt to a boil to create a brine.

• While heating, rinse okra thoroughly. Trim stems if necessary. Pack tightly into a clean glass quart jar. You want to make sure the okra will be covered in brine, so leave a little space at the top and pack the okra tightly so that they will not float to the top. As you pack the okra in, layer the whole garlic cloves, whole dried pepper and whole sprig of dill in the jar as well. Pour boiling water/vinegar mixture over okra in the jar. Cover lightly with lid but leave loose. Let cool on the counter to room temperature. Tighten lid and refrigerate.

Pistachio Watermelon Salad with Jalapeño Orange Balsamic Vinaigrette

Courtesy of Kebabalicious

Kebabalicious is known for their great kebabs and tantalizing ingredient combinations. Here is why. Yield: 4 servings.

10 ounces arugula

1 small seedless watermelon

1 (8-ounce) block of feta (sheep milk)

7 ounces roasted pistachio nuts, chopped

½ red onion sliced thin

10 ounces grape tomatoes

1 bushel fresh mint, diced

Jalapeño Orange Balsamic Vinaigrette:

1 small roasted jalapeño

2 tablespoons Düsseldorf mustard

¼ cup of fresh squeezed navel orange

2½ tablespoons aged balsamic vinegar

1 teaspoon pure wildflower honey

salt and tellecherry pepper to taste

½ cup extra virgin olive oil

• Wash the arugula and find a place to let it dry.

• Take the watermelon and cut it into 1-inch slices (like big discs), then cut those in half. Take a small paring knife and remove the red flesh of the fruit from the green shell. Once complete, cube watermelon into 1-inch pieces and set aside in the refrigerator to chill.

• Cube feta into half-inch bite-size pieces. Set aside.

• Heat a pan, add the chopped pistachio nuts and toast lightly.

• Fill a big bowl with the washed arugula, thinly sliced red onions, grape tomatoes, feta and diced fresh mint. Give it a good toss and put it in the fridge. Let your pistachio nuts cool in pan.

• While that chills, start the dressing. Toast a small

jalapeño over a gas burner until black. Wrap it in saran wrap and let it sweat for about 5 minutes.

• Meanwhile, grab a blender and add the mustard, freshly squeezed orange juice, balsamic, honey, a pinch of kosher salt and tellecherry pepper. Blend until homogenous, and then, very slowly, stream the olive oil into the blender while on low.

• Unwrap the jalapeño and peel off charred outer coating. Cut off the stem and cut jalapeño in half to remove the seeds. Add jalapeño to food processor and liquefy. Taste. Add salt and pepper if needed.

• Take the watermelon out of the fridge and add it to the bowl of salad. Sprinkle your toasted chopped pistachio nuts and serve with the dressing drizzled over or on the side, as you prefer.

Kebabalicious, Chris Childre and Kristian Ulloa

Best friends Chris Childre and Kristian Ulloa grew up in multicultural homes in Houston, Texas. They did their fair share of globe-trotting in their college years. One of the most significant journeys they made was a trip to Switzerland, where they worked for a dynamic Turkish man who taught them the secrets of what would become Kebabalicious. With no European kebabs in Texas, the guys launched their food trailer business and brought it to Austin after graduating from Texas State University in San Marcos.

They are best known for their famous Beef Lamb Kebab, which consists of the traditional beef/lamb shawarma on a warm pita topped with fresh lettuce, tomato, onion, tzatziki and spicy red sauce. Similarly, the Falafel Lebab is smeared with your choice of homemade hummus and then filled with hand-rolled falafels and topped with fresh lettuce, tomatoes, onions, tzatziki and spicy red sauce.

Another fan favorite is their Zucchini Fries. Although they are not readily available (they are the Tuesday special at the lunch stand), they are a rare gluten-free treat. They are made with gluten-free crumbs in a designated gluten-free fryer.

Spring Medley Spinach Salad

Courtesy of Colibri Cuisine

This salad can be adjusted with your favorite seasonal fruits. Colibri Cuisine likes to use a lot of raspberries and blackberries during the spring. When citrus is available, they will also quarter grapefruit and oranges.

½ cup cucumbers, quartered and sliced

1 tablespoon fresh lemon juice

salt, to taste

1 cup fresh organic spinach

1 cup fresh organic spring mix

½ cup shredded or matchstick carrots

½ cup fresh mango, small, diced

½ cup fresh strawberries, sliced finely

½ cup fresh seedless black grapes, quartered

¼ cup almonds, sliced or crumbled (may substitute walnuts)

2 ounces Apple Cider Vinaigrette

• Marinate quartered and sliced cucumbers in lemon juice and salt for ten minutes. Place prepared greens in bowl with carrots. Right before ready to serve, add fruit and cucumbers. Top with almonds. Drizzle on vinaigrette and lemon juice. Toss gently until the dressing lightly coats. Add salt to taste. Arrange carefully on chilled 10.5-inch plate. Finish by adding more nuts or salt on top.

Apple Cider Vinaigrette:

1 part apple cider

½ part olive oil

1 part honey

salt to taste

dab of your favorite salsa (we use sexy roasted chipotle salsa)

• Combine three parts with whisk or emulsifier rapidly until blended well. Add a little salt and a dab of your favorite salsa and continue to mix well. Add salt to taste.

Colibri Cuisine, Anthony Alaniz and Candy Silva

Anthony Alaniz remembers being five years old and begging his grandparents to buy him a special food trailer like the one next door. After leaving a career in accounting and then teaching, he decided to make a go with his own food truck business. "I kept telling my students, 'Follow your dreams, you can be whatever you want to be, stick with it,' and I felt like a hypocrite because I never pursued my own dreams of owning a trailer food business," Anthony shares. He moved from the Rio Grande Valley to Austin to attend culinary school and opened his food trailer.

His fiancée, Candy Silva, was a branch manager for a bank in McAllen, commuting to Austin on the weekends, before moving her family to Austin to support Anthony's dream in the culinary industry. "As a child, my parents were migrant workers, so we traveled a lot to Florida, Michigan and Wisconsin. We picked crops or cleaned fields. I started working and cooking when I was eight years old, helping my parents out in the fields and in our home. As a child, I always tried to help my parents out as much as I could, so I learned how to cook, clean and work quickly. Whenever I could, I would surprise my parents by cooking them dinner," shares Candy.

Candy and Anthony have worked as a team in the trailer for several years. They specialize in fresh Mexican-American cuisine, and their bestseller is their Chicken Quesadillas.

Street Corn

Courtesy of Torchy's Tacos

This hot number was added to the Torchy's menu in 2012. Yield: 4 servings.

4.5 pounds husked corn on the cob

4 ounces mayo or spiced mayo

6 ounces queso fresco

New Mexico red chile powder, for garnish

cilantro, for garnish

• Peel and shuck corn to remove husks. Using a wet paper towel, wipe and peel away remaining strands. Place corn on chargrill on high heat. Turn cobs every 2 minutes until browned and slightly blackened on all sides. Cut corn kernels off cob and set aside.

• Portion every 8 ounces of corn with 1 ounce mayo and 1.5 ounces queso fresco. Garnish with chile powder and cilantro.

Handhelds

The Mickey
Way South Philly

Wow Salad
Sun Farm Kitchen

Bacon Croissant Sandwich
MamboBerry

Brie, Walnut and Honey Sandwich
La Boîte Café

Baja Shrimp Taco
Torchy's Tacos

Banh Mi Taco
The Peached Tortilla

Breaded Pork Tenderloin Sandwich
Tenderland

Hickory-Smoked Pork Loin with Fried
Plantain and Cilantro Pesto
Hey!...You Gonna Eat or What?

Lamb Kebab with Vegan Tzatziki
Sun Farm Kitchen

The Dale Watson Texas Chili Dog
Honky Tonk Hot Dogs

Migas Tacos
Mellizoz Tacos

Pilgrim Turkey Burger with Basil Mayo
Cow Bell's

Pollo Achiote Tacos
La Fantabulous

The Balboa
Way South Philly

The Marciano
Way South Philly

The Cowgirl
Evil Wiener

The Jerk
Snarky's Moo Bawk Oink

The Phat Hawaiian Chicken Cheesesteak
Phatso's Cheesesteaks

The Weldon Henson Spicy Kraut Dog
Honky Tonk Hot Dogs

The Rock Dog
Backstage Grill

The Scott Dog
Honky Tonk Hot Dogs

The Shrimp
Luke's Inside Out

Torta Mexicana
Snarky's Moo Bawk Oink

The Mickey

Courtesy of Way South Philly

A gluten-free option that packs a South Philly punch.
Yield: 2 servings.

44 tater tots

approximately 2 liters vegetable oil

1 medium yellow onion, sliced very thinly (almost shaved) in long strips

1 tablespoon margarine

8 ounces thinly sliced sirloin steak

about ¼ of one red bell pepper, deseeded and cut into ⅛-inch strips

about ¼ of one green bell pepper, deseeded and cut into ⅛-inch strips

Kraft Cheez Whiz

about ¼ of one red bell pepper, deseeded and diced for garnish

about ¼ of one green bell pepper, deseeded and diced for garnish

• Submerge tater tots in vegetable oil for four minutes at 350°F to deep fry them. Bake 'em for a healthier alternative. But what the heck!

• We call our onions "the magic." In order to get the magic right, peel the outer skin of the onion off and discard. Next, cut the onion in half and then cut into very thin strips, almost shaved. To caramelize the onion strips, put them in a tablespoon of margarine over low heat for about three minutes or until they are al dente.

• Sauté 8 ounces thinly sliced sirloin steak with 4 ounces of caramelized onions over medium-low heat to brown each side, about 3 minutes per side. Do not drain the fat! Fat = Flavor.

• In a separate pan, dice and caramelize ¼ red and ¼ green peppers (about 2 ounces of each). Heat about 4 ounces of Kraft Cheez Whiz. When tots are finished cooking, toss immediately with a pinch of sea salt. This helps the salt stick to the tots. Put the tots in a serving container and drizzle 1 ounce of melted Kraft Cheez Whiz over the top. Scoop the steak and onion mixture and dollop a serving on top of Cheez Whiz–smothered tater tots. Garnish with the diced red and green peppers. Put on them boxing gloves, buddy, and get in the ring!

Wow Salad

Courtesy of Sun Farm Kitchen

2–3 cups leafy greens

1 avocado, cubed

1 peach, 1 apple or any
seasonal fruit, diced

¼ cup olives, diced

olive juice, to taste

¼ cup carrots, shredded

¼ cup beets, shredded

1 small handful of sprouts, or
to taste

• Combine all ingredients
except the sprouts and toss
in a large salad bowl. Dress
with your favorite dressing or
eat raw. Add sprouts on top
for an edible garnish.

Sun Farm Kitchen, Kesten Broughton

Prior to opening Sun Farm Kitchens, Kesten Broughton was a video game programmer and farmer. "I opened the trailer to support local farms," shares Kesten authentically. His trailer is located in a community garden that has a live music venue and outdoor art gallery. The crepes on his menu are inspired by his dad, who cooked crepes every Saturday morning while Kesten was growing up in British Columbia, Canada. While the hamburger is his bestseller, it's the lamb kebab with tzatziki that makes Kesten's mouth water.

The trailer food life attracts all kinds. Kesten gives a story about a staffing experience that only a trailer food entrepreneur could embrace: "Once we were slammed during South by Southwest, and a customer, claiming to have five years experience in kitchens, asked if he could help. So he did all our dishes, washed the floor and took inventory in the fridge for us and then took a window shift, heckling some customers for their glitzy cowboy boots."

Bacon Croissant Sandwich

Courtesy of MamboBerry

Bacon, peach jam, brie and basil in an easy-to-make breakfast croissant.

5 pieces thick-cut peppered bacon

1 croissant

3 ounces peach jam (recipe below)

2 ounces soft brie cheese, thinly sliced, with rind removed

8 large finely chopped fresh basil leaves

Quick and Easy Peach Jam:

1 cup diced frozen or fresh peaches

1 teaspoon sugar

¼ teaspoon lemon juice

• Add ingredients to small saucepan and cook uncovered on medium heat for 30 minutes, stirring occasionally.

Sandwich:

• Heat pan to medium high and begin cooking bacon, flipping occasionally. Cook until desired crispness is reached.

• Slice croissant from side to side. In a separate pan, grill croissant on medium heat until crispy, with the inside portions face-down in the pan.

• Heat peach jam in pan or microwave while grilling croissants. Turn over bottom portion of croissant. While still grilling, add brie to crispy part of bottom croissant. Allow to melt for 1 minute. Remove croissants from heat.

• Add peach jam. Add finely chopped basil. Add bacon. Add top portion of croissant. Your sandwich is ready to be enjoyed.

Brie, Walnut and Honey Sandwich

Courtesy of La Boîte Café

A light and easy sandwich to enjoy whiling away the hours, or bring a batch to your next afternoon gathering and share with friends.

French bread

brie

walnuts

honey

arugula

• Cut the French bread into sandwich-sized slices. Slice the brie and slather it on one or both sides of the French bread. Sprinkle some walnuts on one side on top of the brie. Drizzle the honey over the walnuts to glue them onto the sandwich. Put some arugula on top, and you're set.

La Boîte Café, Victoria Davies and Dan Bereczki

Plausibly the most environmentally friendly trailer in Austin, La Boîte Café is an architectural gem that allows patrons to enter and order inside the built-out shipping container. Building your business inside of a repurposed cart is one level of green, but La Boîte utilizes a unique rainwater and purification system within their trailer and also pay close attention to shopping for their food from local Austin farmers.

Victoria Davies and Dan Bereczki met in Austin and designed their European-style trailer business to escape the corporate lifestyle. Their bestsellers are their freshly baked macarons. In particular, the fleur de sel (salted caramel) is a favorite among La Boîte Café regulars.

Baja Shrimp Taco

Courtesy of Torchy's Tacos

Taco lovers will tip their hats to one of Austinites' favorite tacos.
Yield: 4 servings.

½ cup mayonnaise

1 chipotle in adobo, stemmed

½ cup plus 1 tablespoon buttermilk

kosher salt and freshly ground pepper

1½ tablespoons unsalted butter

½ small green cabbage, shredded (about 3 cups)

2 large carrots, shredded

vegetable oil, for frying

24 large shrimp (1¼ pounds), shelled and deveined

2 cups panko (Japanese bread crumbs)

12 corn tortillas, warmed

4 pickled jalapeños, thinly sliced

½ small red onion, thinly sliced

½ cup coarsely chopped cilantro leaves

1½ ounces queso fresco or mild feta, crumbled

lime wedges, for serving four

• In a mini food processor, blend the mayonnaise with the chipotle and 1 tablespoon of buttermilk. Season with salt and pepper and refrigerate.

• Heat a large skillet until very hot. Add the butter, cabbage and carrots and cook over high heat until the cabbage is browned in spots, about 2 minutes. Season with salt and pepper and transfer to a bowl.

• In a large saucepan, heat 2½ inches of vegetable oil to 350°F. In a medium bowl, toss the shrimp with the remaining ½ cup of buttermilk. Put the panko in another bowl. Coat each shrimp with the panko and fry in batches until golden, about 2 minutes per batch. Drain on paper towels.

• Spoon some of the cabbage into the center of each tortilla and top with 2 fried shrimp. Drizzle with the chipotle mayonnaise and sprinkle with some of the pickled jalapeños, red onion, cilantro and queso fresco. Serve with lime wedges.

Torchy's Tacos, Mike Rypka and Partners

Having been a chef at MTV, Dell, Chuys, Lucy's Boat Yard and beyond, Mike Rypka knew what he was doing when he bet his life savings on his green chile pork taco. His consistently good recipes are the reason behind Torchy's rapid success. In addition to their founding trailer where it all began, they now have multiple other brick-and-mortar locations and have expanded into other cities, giving Mike and his partners notoriety as one of the most successful taco trailers in Austin.

Down at the South Austin Trailer Park and Eatery where Torchy's first trailer sits, you can enjoy tacos under the shade of the live oak trees that overlook Bouldin Creek. The names of their tacos are equally shady, with such crowd favorites as the Dirty Sanchez. In addition to their normal menu, you can look for monthly specials like their Turkey Taco with Mole during November.

Banh Mi Taco

Courtesy of The Peached Tortilla

The most popular taco sold on the The Peached Tortilla food truck.
Yield: 12 tacos for four people.

Vietnamese Braised Pork Belly:

3½-pound piece of pork belly

1 tablespoon vegetable oil

Rub:

¼ cup Chinese five-spice

¼ cup brown sugar

kosher salt

black pepper

Braising Liquid:

1 onion, chopped

3 cloves garlic

1/5 cup dark soy

¼ cup light soy

3 pieces star anise

½ cup water

¼ cup rice vinegar

½ cup brown sugar

Preparation—Pork Belly:

• Preheat oven to 350°F. While oven is coming to temp, set your stovetop to high heat and heat vegetable oil in cast-iron skillet. Mix Chinese five-spice, brown sugar, salt and pepper into a dry rub and cover pork belly piece. Make sure to push the rub into the meat. Once the pork belly is covered, sear it in skillet for 4 minutes on each side to ensure that you have sealed in the juices. The pork belly should be nicely browned on each side but not burned. Pull the pork belly out of the skillet and let it rest.

• Without emptying the juices and "bits and ends" from the skillet, sauté onions and garlic for 2 minutes until browned on medium heat. Then add dark soy, star anise, water, rice vinegar and brown sugar. Add pork belly to the braising liquid. The braising liquid should only rise to halfway up the pork belly. Once the oven has reached temperature, place the skillet inside the oven and let it braise for approximately 3½ hours. Pork belly should be very moist and tender, and you should be able to pull it apart with ease. Let pork belly rest after taking it out of the oven, then chop into smaller pieces.

Daikon and Carrot Salad:

½ pound daikon

½ pound carrot, shredded

2–3 tablespoons rice vinegar

2 tablespoons chili garlic

1 tablespoon fish sauce

3 tablespoons sugar, granulated

Preparation—Daikon and Carrot Salad:

• Using Chinese mandolin, julienne daikon and carrot into thin strips. Mix daikon, carrot, rice vinegar, chili garlic, fish sauce and sugar. Let the mixture sit and rest.

Sriracha Mayo:

½ cup mayonnaise

⅛ cup Sriracha

1 tablespoon lemon juice

1 tablespoon rice vinegar

Preparation—Sriracha Mayo:

• Mix mayonnaise, Sriracha, lemon juice and rice vinegar together and place into a squeeze bottle.

Additional Ingredients:

tortillas (flour or corn), 5 inch

cilantro, chopped

Assembly:

• Heat tortillas on griddle or stovetop, then add pork belly to fill the tortilla. Top with daikon/carrot mixture, Sriracha mayo to taste and cilantro to garnish.

The Peached Tortilla, Eric Silverstein

What makes an attorney quit a successful litigation practice and move across the country to open a food truck? That is precisely what entrepreneur Eric Silverstein did when he moved from Missouri to Austin to open The Peached Tortilla. "After I went to law school, I was a litigator for three years. I didn't love my job; I was looking to do something else. I'd been working on this idea for a long time and decided the food truck is what I wanted to do next. I quit my job, moved three weeks later and started The Peached Tortilla," explains Eric.

Born in Japan, Eric had been exposed to the different food cultures of China, Bali and Singapore as he traveled around Asia with his parents. When his family moved to Atlanta at age ten, he began eating the different flavors of the South. "When I started The Peached Tortilla concept, it made sense to mingle those two (Asian flavors with southern flavors). The name originates from my Georgia roots because it's the Peach State. We want people to 'get peached,' or flavor-smitten, with our tacos," shares the ex-attorney cum chef.

Known around town for his pork banh mis and his bacon jam, Eric went from starting a business to becoming one of the most sought-after food trucks in the business. Although his professional background is in law, Eric started washing dishes for Einstein Bros. Bagels when he was sixteen and has worked at different restaurants. Perhaps the restaurant business is in his DNA. Eric's father has spent a lifetime in the food business consulting for restaurant chains and owns two restaurants in Hong Kong.

Tenderland, Angela Springer and Jeremy Newlin

The idea of Tenderland surfaced one night when brother and sister Jeremy and Angela were trying to choose a spot to meet for dinner with their families. It was Jeremy whose mind drifted to a huge battered pork tenderloin sandwich like the ones they used to make back home in Iowa. "Pork tenderloins are as popular in Iowa as tacos are in Texas," shares Angela. Like brothers and sisters are prone to do, the conversation shifted into a competition as to who could make the best breaded pork tenderloin sandwich. The troops headed to the grocery store for supplies, and at the end of a home-cooked family meal, it was decided that they would start Tenderland.

Their Big As a Plate Battered Pork Tenderloin is not only a family favorite but also their bestseller. It starts with six to eight ounces of pork, straight from the loin, pounded flat, hand breaded and deep-fried in peanut oil. It is served with homemade chipotle mayo, ketchup, mustard, pickles, onions and jalapeños.

You'll find a very eclectic crowd on Tenderland's benches on any given day. "Our customers are from all walks of life: students, families, etc. We have a local group from a nearby company that all come together on a weekly basis and have for almost as long as we've been open. We have another group that call themselves the Senior Birthday Celebration Group from a city north of Austin. They get dressed up in party hats and can make the younger generations proud by their celebratory style," shares Angela of her customers.

Breaded Pork Tenderloin Sandwich

Courtesy of Tenderland

Pork tenderloin sandwiches are as common in Iowa as tacos are in Texas. This brother-and-sister food truck team brought their favorite food from back home in Iowa to their new home in Austin, Texas.

oil, for frying

1 cup breading, such as cornmeal or panko bread crumbs

1 cup salted crackers, such as saltines, crushed

1 teaspoon salt

1 teaspoon freshly ground pepper

your favorite seasoning, such as garlic or onion powder (optional)

1–2 cups milk

2–4 large eggs, beaten

4–6 boneless pork chops, excess fat trimmed

your favorite buns, for serving

• Heat oil to 350°F in a large pot.

• Mix together the breading, crackers, salt, pepper and your favorite seasoning in a large bowl. Whisk together the milk and eggs in a separate large bowl.

• Pound the pork ⅛- to ¼-inch thin (thickness is purely a personal preference) using a meat mallet. Dip the pork into the egg batter and then immediately coat with the breading mixture.

• Deep-fry the pork until the middle is white when cut open, approximately 4 to 6 minutes. Let the oil drain off before placing on buns. Dress the sandwich to your preference with mayonnaise, ketchup, mustard, pickles, onions or jalapeños.

Hickory-Smoked Pork Loin with Fried Plantain and Cilantro Pesto

Courtesy of Hey!...You Gonna Eat or What?

This sandwich featuring pork and plantains throws a chin nod to traditional Cuban cuisine. The multipurpose Cilantro Pesto brings in light, earthy and herbal tones.

6-inch ciabatta

1 tablespoon extra-virgin olive oil

2 quarts canola oil for deep frying

½ plantain, bisected length-wise and cut into 2½-inch pieces

3 thick-cut slices hickory-smoked pork loin

2 tablespoons Cilantro Pesto

green leaf lettuce

Cilantro Pesto:

½ cup pan-roasted pine nuts

1½ cups packed cilantro, large stems removed

½ cup packed Italian parsley, large stems removed

½ cup grated Parmesan cheese

½ cup grated Romano cheese

1 teaspoon freshly ground sea salt

¼ cup extra-virgin olive oil

1 teaspoon lemon juice

Preparing the Cilantro Pesto:

• In a frying pan over medium heat, pan-roast the ½ cup of pine nuts for 90 seconds to 2 minutes or until slightly tanned. Combine all ingredients into a blender and blend on a medium setting until the pesto has a smooth consistency. Refrigerate until ready to use.

Assembling the Sandwich:

• Cut your ciabatta to accommodate a 6-inch sandwich and then bisect laterally. Pan-toast the bread with a tablespoon of extra-virgin olive oil. Once toasted, remove bread to dress.

• Heat fryer to 355°F and, once heated, fry 4 pieces of plantain for 3 to 4 minutes (or until slightly tanned). Once fried, remove from oil and transfer to heated pan with residual olive oil from bread.

• Sear 3 slices of pork loin for 3 minutes, flipping them after 90 seconds. Once flipped, generously baste the pork loin slices with Cilantro Pesto.

• Spread Cilantro Pesto on both the top and bottom slices of your baguette. Transfer the basted pork loin from the pan to the bottom slice of bread and spread out, slightly overlapping one another. Next, remove your 4 slices of plantain and stack them on top of the pork loin. Finish sandwich with two generous leaves of green leaf lettuce and top the sandwich with your top slice of ciabatta. Voila!

Hey!…You Gonna Eat or What? Eric Regan and Lizziane "Liz" Abreu-Regan

With over twenty years of working in the fine dining industry under his belt, Eric Regan decided what many food truck entrepreneurs decide: it was time to start working for himself. "I've been working long and hard hours for years as a restaurant GM. Now I am still working hard…But it's for me!" Eric says as he smiles.

Eric's menu revolves around a thick Austin slant poured over traditional American sandwiches. For example, his spin on the Monte Cristo is a Shiner Bock (local) beer-battered sandwich with homemade cherry/fig jelly. "We use a Shiner Bock beer batter to compliment the smoked meats in the sandwich: mesquite-smoked turkey and hickory-smoked ham. We also love the pairing of our cherry and fig jelly with the cheeses in the sandwich: mild cheddar and provolone," explains the chef.

Attention to the customer is part of the experience guests receive when they eat at the red-hot 1974 Argosy trailer. The really incredible food has folks driving in from all over the state, but Eric claims it's their service that the guests find refreshing. "My background is in fine dining. In a lot of ways, I employ fine dining protocol in the way we assist our guests and in the way we serve them their food. I began describing the food in detail to the guests early on in our storied history, and it resonated with people. They love having the chef walk them through what he's done for them. What's more, they see how much pride we take in producing our dishes," says Eric.

Lamb Kebab with Vegan Tzatziki

Courtesy of Sun Farm Kitchen

You'll never know this full-flavored Tzatziki is vegan.

mushrooms

lamb from Locinto's, cubed and marinated in garlic and red wine

Tzatziki (see below)

• Place alternating mushrooms and lamb on skewer and grill until meat is thoroughly cooked. Make the Tzatziki for a dipping sauce.

Tzatziki:

3 cloves of garlic

2 cucumbers

fresh dill from the garden

1 part vegan sour cream

1 part vegan mayonnaise

2 tablespoons lemon juice

salt and pepper to taste

• Crush the garlic. Optionally, peel the cucumber and cut into chunks. Add all ingredients together in food processor and blend until smooth.

Take care not to over blend, which will cause the mixture to be runny.

The Dale Watson Texas Chili Dog

Courtesy of Honky Tonk Hot Dogs

A nod to the famous Texas musician, the Dale Watson is a crowd pleaser.

Vienna beef hot dog

hoagie bun, buttered and toasted

spicy mustard, to taste

shredded cheddar cheese, to taste

homemade Texas-style chili, to taste

chopped onion, to taste

jalapeños, to taste

• This luscious dog starts with a Vienna beef hot dog, boiled for 4 minutes and then grilled for 30 seconds. Place the grilled dog in a buttery toasted petite hoagie bun that is lined to perfection with spicy mustard and shredded cheddar cheese and topped with homemade Texas-style chili (no beans!), chopped onion and jalapeños.

Migas Tacos

Courtesy of Mellizoz Tacos

A traditional breakfast meal in Austin; you can't go wrong with the Migas Tacos.
Yield: 3 servings.

1 Roma tomato

⅛ cup white or yellow onion, diced

1 clove garlic, minced

½ jalapeño pepper, seeded and minced

2 sprigs cilantro

1 tablespoon lemon juice

kosher salt, to taste

fresh cracked pepper, to taste

3 yellow corn tortillas

4 tablespoons oil

4 eggs, scrambled

shredded cheddar cheese

• Start by making pico de gallo—a simple salsa that means "beak of the rooster" in Spanish. Dice up the Roma tomato and onion, crush and mince the garlic, mince the jalapeño pepper and remove the seeds (unless you like it spicy!) and add the cilantro, lemon juice and salt and pepper to taste. Set aside and reserve for later.

• Dice the yellow corn tortillas into 1-inch squares and heat the oil in a pan until just before it begins to smoke. Gently toss in the "chips" and sauté until crispy and toasty. Drain any excess oil.

• Add about 2–3 tablespoons of the pico de gallo to the pan. After sauteing the pico with the chips until the veggies have slightly caramelized, it's time to add the eggs. Gently pour the four scrambled eggs over the chip and pico mixture. Season with salt and pepper to your liking. Stir the egg mixture evenly until you get the eggs to the proper doneness, being careful not to overcook the eggs.

• Turn off the heat and then sprinkle in the cheddar cheese, allowing it to melt over the cooked egg mixture.

• Plate and serve with additional corn or flour tortillas and the remaining pico de gallo. Alternatively, include refried or charro beans and roasted potatoes to accompany the dish, or just wrap them in a few tortillas and take them on the go.

Mellizoz Tacos, John Galindo

"Where good friends make tacos and good tacos make friends."

Being a fourth-generation Austinite with a family history in the restaurant business, John Galindo is a hometown hero. Austinites will recognize his great-grandfather's efforts in working to open the iconic Tavern on 11th and Lamar, and his grandmother used to waitress at Jaime's Spanish Village. In fact, there are over one hundred years of combined experience in the food service industry working in the Izzoz trailer today. *Mellizoz* is a shortened word in Spanish for twins. Since twins run in the Galindo family and John has niece and nephew twins, the name Izzoz made sense.

Having cooked with some of the best, John's food certainly stands out, as does his customer service. He calls you his guest, never a "customer," and goes out of his way to remember your name and what you like to be sure to put a smile on your face the next time you visit his establishment. Having been rooted in the business for so long, he has some suggestions for new vendors: "It's not what you're selling, it's how you sell it— it's the same with tacos or cupcakes or pies or stuff in a cone—attention to detail. The character you bring every day is what matters."

Pilgrim Turkey Burger with Basil Mayo

Courtesy of Cow Bell's

Fancy up your fall tailgating by grilling this turkey burger with dried cranberries and basil mayonnaise.
Yield: 4 quarter-pound burgers.

1 pound ground turkey

1 tablespoon soy sauce

1 teaspoon black pepper

1 teaspoon minced onion

1 teaspoon olive oil

1½ teaspoons garlic powder

¼ cup parsley

steak seasoning, to taste

4 whole wheat buns

2–3 tablespoons butter, as needed

Basil Mayo (recipe below)

dried cranberries, a few to taste

lettuce

tomato

• In a large bowl, mix together turkey, soy sauce, black pepper, minced onion, olive oil, garlic powder and parsley. Place turkey mixture in a separate container and let it sit in the fridge for an hour.

• Remove turkey from the container and form into four ½-inch-thick patties. When the grill is ready and hot, cook turkey burgers 4 minutes and 47 seconds on each side, flipping only once. While cooking, hit each side of the burger with a sprinkle of steak seasoning.

• Lightly butter and toast buns on the grill, approximately 30 seconds on each side. Dress the top bun with Basil Mayo and a few dried cranberries. Add fresh green leaf lettuce and a thick tomato slice and you're good to go!

Basil Mayo:

Yield: 1 cup

1 cup mayonnaise

½ tablespoon fresh basil leaves

1 teaspoon lemon olive oil

• Mix all ingredients in a small bowl and whisk until blended.

Cow Bell's, Daniel and Lourdes Oliveira

"I started working at my uncle Carlos's restaurant when I was sixteen years old so I could pay for gas and go to the movies. I started as a busboy wiping down tables and throwing out the trash. Gradually, I started doing the register, then the fryer and the burgers. Once I was there for a few years, I became a manager. It was great working for my uncle and his crew, but eventually I wanted to do something a little bit different. I love to cook people food. It makes me feel good. I was in the restaurant business for years and was longing for something fun like this. It was time to pull the trigger and give it a shot!" shares owner Daniel Olieveira about opening his burger joint.

After he graduated from high school, Daniel's uncle Carlos bought him an Old Smokey charcoal grill. "They're very basic but awesome to cook on! My uncle Carlos showed me the ropes on a couple different cuts of meat, and the rest is history. He also didn't forget to teach me that a couple ice cold Budweisers was a great way to prime the engine before a big feast," smiles Daniel as he talks about his uncle.

The name Cow Bell's came from an old *Saturday Night Live* skit with Will Farrell and Christopher Walken. After nine to ten months of researching and planning, the food trailer became a reality. Daniel's mother, Lourdes, takes care of the numbers and shopping, while he does the grilling and frying at the trailer. "All in all, we make a pretty good team," says Daniel.

The Blue Flame is the bestseller. It's a burger dressed with blue cheese, grilled jalapeños, lettuce and tomato. The Boca Chicas sliders are another favorite: they come on Hawaiian sweet rolls with ketchup, pickles and grilled onions.

You meet some interesting folks out on the street. Daniel shares about one of his good customers: "There's this one man who walks by the trailer on a daily basis. It's a little random, but he always brings me a one-liter Dr. Pepper. After he comes through a few times, I hook him up with a hamburger. Win-win situation."

Pollo Achiote Tacos

Courtesy of La Fantabulous

These are Josie's bestsellers and her personal favorite item on the menu.

6 tablespoons extra-virgin olive oil

1 pound boneless, skinless chicken breasts

salt, pepper and cumin to taste

1 large yellow onion, thinly sliced

1 cup fresh pineapple, diced small

4 ounces Rogelio Bueno achiote sauce (Annatto Condiment)

12 corn tortillas

½ cup queso fresco, crumbled

1 bushel cilantro, chopped, for garnish

• Heat 3 tablespoons of olive oil in a large skillet. Season the chicken all over with salt, pepper and cumin, then add the chicken to the skillet and cook over moderately high heat, turning once, until browned, about 6 to 8 minutes, depending on size of chicken breast. Transfer chicken to a dish; let cool.

• When chicken has cooled, cut into small dices. Add the remaining 3 tablespoons of olive oil to the skillet, along with the onion. Cook over moderately high heat, stirring occasionally, until the onion is lightly browned and softened, approximately 5 minutes. Add the diced chicken and pineapple; cook until pineapple is lightly browned, approximately three minutes. Add the achiote sauce and cook until fragrant, stirring occasionally, approximately 5 minutes.

• Warm the corn tortillas and spoon about 2 to 3 tablespoons of chicken onto each tortilla. Sprinkle with questo fresco and cilantro.

La Fantabulous, Josie Paredes

Josie Paredes had been cooking since she was seven, and she spent twenty-five years in commercial kitchens before opening her taqueria trailer in 2007. "First of all, I am Mexican. Food trailers and street food are very normal for me," shares Josie. "I grew up going to visit my grandparents in Mexico every chance I could get, and they had a mini market food stand where my aunts cooked in the open for customers. Eventually, they built their own food trailer. Like them, having a food trailer of my own was definitely a goal."

Her menu is also inspired from hole-in-the-wall places she visited while backpacking the beaches in Mexico. "I love the way they combine their seasons with their fresh meat and fruits, and a lot of avocado," Josie says. Josie's mother can take credit for giving her the passion to cook. Josie says, "My mom made her moles from scratch. She used different dried peppers, peanut butter and chocolate. What's not to love—it's Reese's Pieces on chicken."

Not only is cooking for others in her blood, but it's also part of her résumé. Josie has had the pleasure of working with several esteemed restaurants and companies around the country. She was the only female hire at the original downtown Eddie Vs location, and she helped develop the Santa Rita Mexican food concept in Austin, Texas. While on the East Coast, she worked as a pastry chef for McCormick & Schmick's. Upon her return to Austin, Josie worked for several other notable restaurants and helped develop the concept behind J Black's Feel Good Kitchen and Lounge.

The best part of the trailer food business for Josie, like many other food trailer entrepreneurs, is that she gets to see someone smile because of something she cooked. "I get to do my own thing. I love to cook. I like to make people happy with my food. I love the expression. That's the best payment for me, that someone else is enjoying something I made out of love."

The Balboa

Courtesy of Way South Philly

This is a traditional South Philly cheesesteak. Yield: 4.

1 medium yellow onion, sliced very thinly (almost shaved) in long strips

1 tablespoon margarine

16 ounces sirloin steak, thinly sliced

salt and pepper to taste

4 Philly rolls or your favorite sub roll

Kraft Cheez Whiz

• We call our onions "the magic." In order to get the magic right, peel the outer skin of the onion off and discard. Next, cut the onion in half and then cut into very thin strips, almost shaved. To caramelize the onion strips, put them in a tablespoon of margarine over low heat for about three minutes or until they are al dente.

• Sauté the thinly sliced sirloin steak along with the caramelized onions over medium-low heat to brown each side, about 3 minutes per side. Do not drain the fat! Fat = Flavor. Add salt and pepper to taste.

• Next, get some REAL Philly rolls (or your favorite sub roll), slice them down the center and toast for a second or two. Spread Kraft Cheez Whiz all over the inside of the rolls; pile the steak and onion mixture in between the bread.

• Squeeze gently; lean forward so the back end of the sandwich points away from you. Have napkins ready! If prepared correctly, it's gonna get messy.

Way South Philly, Willy Pearce and Richard Briglia Jr.

After Willy Pearce was laid off due to the economy, he decided he wanted to make authentic cheesesteaks in Austin. From concept to realization, it took him and his brother about forty-five days to open Way South Philly in East Austin. Their menu is *Rocky* (the movie) themed, with items like the Balboa, which is their top-selling cheesesteak. It contains a generous portion of seasoned grilled Philly steak, sautéed with steamed onions then topped with Cheez Wiz on a Philadelphia-made roll.

Willy offers more than your average food truck. "All staff are ordained, so we can do walk-up weddings or vow renewals. The Wedding Special is two soft drinks, two tater tots, two cheesesteaks and a wedding or vow renewal ceremony for $59.99," shares Willy. They also have a food challenge called the Italian Stallion: "Equal to four Balboas but with more, the Italian Stallion is a huge roll overflowing with Philly steak, peppers, onions, mushrooms, tots, then smothered with Cheez Wiz. If you finish this sandwich yourself in twelve rounds (that's thirty-six minutes), you will be crowned a champ, go on the wall of fame and get to create and name a cheesesteak that will go on the menu," Willy explains.

The Marciano

Courtesy of Way South Philly

This is a traditional South Philly pizza steak. Yield: 4.

1 medium yellow onion

1 red bell pepper, deseeded and cut into ⅛-inch strips

1 green bell pepper, deseeded and cut into ⅛-inch strips

1 tablespoon margarine

16 ounces sirloin steak, thinly sliced

salt and pepper to taste

4 Philly rolls, or your favorite sub roll

8 slices of smoked provolone (or, as we say, "provy")

approximately 8 ounces of your favorite red pizza sauce

dried oregano and dried basil

• Just like in the Balboa, you'll need to start with "the magic" (onions). In order to get the magic right, peel the outer skin of the onion off and discard. Next, cut the onion in half and then cut into very thin strips, almost shaved. Combine onion with bell pepper strips and caramelize by sautéing them in a tablespoon of margarine over low heat for about 3 minutes or until they are al dente.

• Sauté 16 ounces thinly sliced sirloin steak with the caramelized onions and peppers over medium-low heat to brown each side, about 3 minutes per side. Do not drain the fat! Fat = Flavor. Add salt and pepper to taste.

• Get some REAL Philly rolls, slice down the center and toast for a second or two. Place 2 slices of provy inside the roll. Add about 6 ounces of peppers, onions and steak mixture on top of the provy inside the Philly roll. Top with a dollop of your favorite red pizza sauce and sprinkle a pinch of dried oregano and dried basil right on top. Squeeze gently; lean forward so the back end of the sandwich points away from you. Have napkins ready! If prepared correctly, it's gonna get messy.

The Cowgirl

Courtesy of Evil Wiener

A bona fide Texas BBQ meets an American tradition: the hot dog.

¼ cup smoked brisket, chopped

1 Vienna beef wiener

1–2 tablespoons vegetable oil, as needed

1 seeded wiener bun

BBQ sauce

shredded iceberg or romaine lettuce

sliced onions

sliced dill pickles

• Warm up about ¼ cup brisket and add a squirt of water and a pinch of salt to moisten and season. Cook the wiener in a pan with a few drops of oil and slowly brown on low heat.

• Toast the bun. When both meats are heated through, place the brisket in the bun and then lay the wiener on top. Drizzle with BBQ sauce.

• Add the shredded iceberg, sliced onions and sliced pickles and drizzle with BBQ sauce one more time.

If you want to smoke your own brisket like they do at Evil Wiener:

10 to 12 pounds brisket, untrimmed

sea salt, to season

fresh cracked black pepper, to season

granulated garlic, to season

• Have a smoker ready at 225° to 250°F. Season brisket with sea salt, pepper and garlic. Place the brisket on the grates, fat side up, away from the coals. Cook for about 15 hours at the constant temperature listed. Add more wood as needed to keep the coals glowing. The internal temperature of the brisket should be about 190°F when done. If you want, you can wrap with foil halfway through the cooking process to help with moistness if you are a novice smoker. Let the meat rest for about 30 minutes before using.

Evil Wiener, Jeff Cummins, Roger Zapata and Their Families

Although at different times and different institutions, both Jeff Cummins and Roger Zapata graduated from culinary school in California. They met when working together at a local Austin restaurant and determined they had a lot in common. With twenty-five years of combined experience, the two friends sat down over beers and hatched a plan to open the Evil Wiener.

Putting their passions and priorities in line with family and food (in that order), Evil Wiener began to roam the streets serving glorified hot dogs. Their families all get involved and help with every aspect of their food trailer business. They love eating, drinking and serving food to different communities in Austin.

"Life in a food truck is not one that lacks complexity. Repeated generator problems, finding accounts, an ever-evolving menu, customer service, exhausting days, social media, website, unexpected expenses, rainy days, insurance, food costs, attorneys' fees, CPAs' fees, bookkeeping, winging it, losing it and just simply staying sane without losing the love of our craft!" So goes part of the story line with the Evil Wiener through Jeff's wife, Anna, who does the marketing and media for the food truck.

Snarky's Moo Bawk Oink, Chuck Watkins and Robert Higgs

"I had a background in restaurant ownership and management, and Rob is in construction. We wanted to start a trailer concept and also a destination for North Austin trailer food, so we started the NATY (North Austin Trailer Yard). We have been friends for thirty years and went to Anderson High School together. We both grew up in North Austin, so it made sense to try and bring the trailer concept to the area where we grew up," shares Chuck.

Chuck Watkins and Rob Higgs bought a 1991 Austin Independent School District school bus from Craigslist. Rob's construction background came in handy when it was time to repurpose the bus into a mobile kitchen.

Chuck, of course, developed the sandwich menu, which allows you to choose your preference of meat: beef (moo), chicken (bawk) or pork (oink). They use well-seasoned, tender meat as a base and differentiate each of the sandwiches with signature sauces, spices and ingredients.

The Snarky Cheesesteak is their top seller. It comes with a choice of beef, chicken or pork with grilled onions, jack cheese, sweet caramelized jalapeños and Snarky Sauce (homemade spicy honey mustard). But the Pig in a Prom Dress is Chuck's personal favorite: slow-roasted pork, bacon and ham, grilled with onion and jack cheese and finished with peach habanero jelly.

The Jerk

Courtesy of Snarky's Moo Bawk Oink

The Jerk is a delicious sandwich with slo-roasted meat with jerk seasoning and pineapple slaw.

toasted baguette

slow-roasted meat [beef (moo), chicken (bawk) OR pork (oink)]

jerk rub—season meat while grilling (13 different spices)

2 ounces Pineapple Slaw

Slaw:

1 cup mayo

2 tablespoons apple cider vinegar

1 tablespoon black pepper

1 teaspoon garlic

2 teaspoons celery salt

2½ pounds shredded cabbage and carrot coleslaw mix

- Combine first 5 ingredients in a bowl and mix well. Pour mixture on top of slaw mix and toss until blended.

Jerk Dry Rub:

5 teaspoons allspice

2 teaspoons thyme

2 teaspoons ginger

2 teaspoons nutmeg

2 teaspoons cinnamon

2 teaspoons cayenne

1 teaspoon crushed red pepper

1 teaspoon black [epper

4 teaspoons fine sea salt

4 teaspoons sugar

3 teaspoons garlic

1 teaspoon ground cloves

2 teaspoons onion powder

- Mix all ingredients together until well blended.

Slow-Roasted Pork:

- Season boneless/skinless chicken thigh meat with a dry rub of salt, pepper, garlic and paprika to taste. Slow cook the meat with 2 cups of water in a Crock-Pot (high for 2½ hours), roasting pan in oven (250°F for 2½ hours) or in a pressure cooker (high for 50 minutes). Once cooked, shred and let cool.

Pineapple Slaw:

2 ounces pineapple tidbits, drained

½ teaspoon fresh diced jalapeños

½ teaspoon Jerk Dry Rub

- Mix all ingredients together.

Assembly:

- On a griddle or in a pan (medium high heat), place the pineapple slaw (juice and all) in the pan, add cooked chicken and sprinkle to taste with Dry Jerk Rub. Heat for forty-five to sixty seconds, then turn over and mix together. Top the mixture with ⅓ cup slaw; sprinkle with dry rub again. Place mixture into a lightly toasted baguette. Serve remaining slaw as a side dish.

The Phat Hawaiian Chicken Cheesesteak

Courtesy of Phatso's Cheesesteaks

Cheesesteak in paradise.

2 small cans crushed pineapple

⅓ cup soy sauce

2 tablespoons vegetable oil

⅓ cup honey

¼ cup rice wine vinegar

3 cloves garlic, minced

1 tablespoon fresh ginger, grated

1 half cup clarified butter

1 (8-inch) Amoroso's Italian hoagie roll or comparable crusty roll

1 boneless skinless chicken breast

½ yellow South Texas 10/15 onion, diced

1 can chunk pineapple

1–2 slices thin-sliced deli-style provolone cheese

2 slices Canadian bacon

- In a large Ziploc bag, combine crushed pineapple, soy sauce, vegetable oil, honey, rice wine vinegar, garlic and ginger. Zip bag and shake to mix. Add chicken. Close bag and massage marinade into chicken. Place in refrigerator and marinate for six hours. After marinating, cube chicken.

- In a large frying pan, add 2 tablespoons of clarified butter and lightly brown Amoroso's roll on both sides. Then add 2 to 3 tablespoons of clarified butter, diced onions and 8 to 10 pineapple chunks. Cook onions/pineapple on medium-high heat, approximately 3 to 5 minutes. When onions turn opaque in color, add cubed chicken breast. When chicken is thoroughly cooked, toss with onions and pineapple.

- Top off sizzling mixture with 1 to 2 slices of provolone cheese. When cheese melts, immediately remove and place mixture on top of your warm, buttery Amoroso's roll. Top off with two slices of lightly browned Canadian bacon.

Phatso's Cheesesteaks, Walter Underwood

Walter Underwood's grandparents owned the Underwood Café in Brownsville, Texas, during the Great Depression. It was in Brownsville where Walter sold his own brick-and-mortar restaurant in order to be able to return to Austin. He saw opening a food trailer as the fastest way to get back in business and opened Phatso's in April 2012.

Born in Bryn Mawr, Pennsylvania, just outside Philly, Walter knows what constitutes a really great cheesesteak. Once working as a registered nurse grew tiresome, he made the leap to start his own cheesesteak business. He imports authentic rolls from Amoroso's Bakery in Philadelphia, and the Queso Steak is his bestseller. The Phat Hawaiian is Walter's personal favorite with chicken, Canadian bacon and a pineapple marinade.

The Weldon Henson Spicy Kraut Dog

Courtesy of Honky Tonk Hot Dogs

Folks like to swing, two-step, waltz and even polka to Weldon's honky-tonk music.

Vienna beef hot dog

grilled sauerkraut, to taste

grilled jalapeños, to taste

spicy mustard, to taste

petite hoagie bun

• Boil a Vienna beef hot dog for 4 minutes and grill for 30 seconds. Cover it with grilled kraut and jalapeños topped with spicy mustard. Serve on a buttery toasted, spicy mustard–caramelized petite hoagie bun.

The Rock Dog

Courtesy of Backstage Grill

The Backstage Grill supports local 512-Austin artists and names their gourmet bar food after famous musicians.

1 Smokey Denmark's Jalapeño Smoked Sausage

1 slice applewood smoked bacon

1 Mexican bolillo roll

1 tablespoon Mango Pico de Gallo

1 tablespoon Pineapple Guacamole

1 ounce crumbled queso fresco

few sprigs cilantro

2 ounces of your favorite chipotle aioli or spiced mayonnaise

• Prepare grill to medium heat. Partially cook bacon, 2 to 3 minutes. Wrap each sausage with the partially cooked bacon using toothpicks. Place sausages on the grill and cook for only 2 to 3 minutes a side. Grill until the bacon is cooked, then remove from the grill and remove the toothpicks.

• Slice bolillo roll in half and toast on grill, then top with Mango Pico de Gallo and the Pineapple Guacamole, equally. Then sprinkle with queso fresco and a few sprigs of cilantro. Finish with Chipotle Aioli and enjoy.

Mango Pico de Gallo:

¼ cup mango

¼ cup red onion

¼ cup tomato

¼ cup minced garlic

1 ounce chopped cilantro

2 ounces fresh squeezed lime juice

1 pinch salt

Pineapple Guacamole:

2 ripe avocados

¼ cup fresh pineapple

¼ cup red onion

¼ cup tomatoe

¼ cup minced garlic

1 ounce chopped cilantro

2 ounces fresh squeezed lime juice

1 pinch salt

The Scott Dog

Courtesy of Honky Tonk Hot Dogs

> *This is a Chicago-inspired dog with a Texas twist.*

Vienna beef hot dog

dill relish, to taste

chopped onions, to taste

2 tomato wedges

pickled jalapeño pepper rings, to taste

yellow mustard, to taste

pickle spear

celery salt, to taste

dash of chili powder

petite hoagie bun

- Boil a Vienna beef hot dog for 4 minutes and grill for 30 seconds. Cover it with dill relish, chopped onions, tomato wedges, pickled jalapeño pepper rings, yellow mustard, a pickle spear and celery salt…with a dash of chili powder! Serve on a buttery toasted petite hoagie bun.

Honky Tonk Hot Dogs, Scott Angle

Scott Angle didn't exactly have culinary experience before he started his own food trailer business. Prior to opening Honky Tonk Hot Dogs out of a converted horse trailer, Scott had worked all of one shift at Denny's while attending college. "I am a country musician in Austin; I'm also part of the dancing scene. I thought I'd start a business that could bring together my love for music, my friends and good food. I have built a dance floor around my trailer, and I frequently have live country music acts," says Scott.

He names all his dogs after local country music celebrities: Dale Watson, Cindy Cashdollar, Redd Voelkeart, etc. Most of the musicians have stopped by at least once to see what their dog is all about. The Scott Dog is his namesake. "I lived in Chicago for fourteen years, so I took the traditional Chicago-style dog and put a Texas twist on it," he explains.

The Shrimp

Courtesy of Luke's Inside Out

One of the trailer's most popular sandwiches, as featured on the Food Network's Diners, Drive-Ins and Dives.

Bleu Goo:

16 ounces crumbled blue cheese

2 ounces honey

16 ounces mayonnaise

1 ounce whole-grain Dijon mustard

- Whisk ingredients together to combine.

shrimp patty, cooked

toasted French bread

1 ounce baby spinach

½ green apple, chopped

½ ounce sliced red onion

- Assemble the shrimp sandwich by placing a shrimp patty on a piece of toasted French bread. Add about three ounces of Bleu Goo, spinach, apple and onion. Grab a napkin.

Luke's Inside Out, Luke Bibby

Luke Bibby has served his creative menu to Willie Nelson over thirty times, and the list of accomplished musicians he has served is impressive: ZZ Top, Crosby, Stills and Nash, Beck, the Allman Brothers, Asleep at the Wheel, Lyle Lovett, Tool, Joan Baez, Outkast, Snoop Dogg, Steve Earl and more. After a lifetime of serving musicians his out-there cuisine, as Luke calls it, he opened a trailer due to popular demand.

Anything Luke cooks has a uniquely Luke touch. The Shrimp sandwich and the Korean rabbit with Tater Tots sandwich were two favorites of the *Diners, Drive-Ins and Dives* crew that came to film him at his trailer with Guy Fieri. His watermelon wedge contains feta, rosemary and Pop Rocks. Try any of his "traiolees" for some special sauce on anything you eat from his trailer.

Torta Mexicana

Courtesy of Snarky's Moo Bawk Oink

This sandwich, or torta, is made on a light baguette and pressed like a Cuban sandwich. Snarky's also recommends adding guacamole. The Torta Mexicana is great with pork, but Snarky's concept allows the choice of beef (moo) chicken (bawk) or pork (oink), so pick whichever meat best suits your taste buds.

Slow-Roasted Pork

2 ounces Snarky's Black Beans

2 ounces Snarky's Pickled Habanero Red Onions

2 slices monterey jack cheese

toasted baguette

Slow-Roasted Pork:

• Cut boneless pork shoulder in 2-inch cubes and season with a dry rub of salt, pepper, garlic and paprika to taste. Sear on high heat on griddle or in a sauté pan, approximately 4 minutes on each side, to form a thin cooked layer all around the meat. This will seal in the juices as the meat is slow cooked. Next, slow cook the meat with 2 cups of water in a Crock-Pot (high for 4 hours), roasting pan in oven (250°F for 4 hours) or in a pressure cooker (high for 70 minutes). Once cooked, shred and let cool.

Snarky's Black Beans:

1 gallon cooked black beans

4 cups chipotle in adobo pureed

1 cup fresh jalapeño (finely diced)

1 cup chopped cilantro

½ cup fresh lime juice

• Mix all ingredients together and refrigerate overnight.

Snarky's Pickled Habanero Red Onions:

5 pounds diced red onion

½ gallon water

2 cups white vinegar

1 tablespoon black pepper

2 teaspoons cumin

1 teaspoon Mexican oregano

1 teaspon garlic powder

2 tablespons sugar

2 teaspoons salt

3 pierced habaneros

• Bring all contents to a boil and cook for 15 minutes while stirring. Remove habaneros and refrigerate overnight.

Assembly:

• On a griddle or in a pan (medium-high heat), heat Slow-Roasted Pork, placing Snarky's Black Beans and Pickled Habanero Red Onions on top of meat. Let heat for 45 to 60 seconds, turn over and mix together. Add sliced jack cheese on top and let melt. Place mixture into a light baguette, wrap in foil and press on grill with large/heavy cast-iron pan.

Dinners

Gluten-Free Vegetable Lasagna
Snap Pod

Beef (or Lamb) with Prunes
The Flying Carpet

Bourbon Braised Pork Shoulder with Cream Corn
Seedling Truck

Bufalo Bob's Shrimp Creole
Bufalo Bob's Chalupa Wagon

Butternut Squash Ravioli with Fontina Cheese Veloute
Regal Ravioli

Dr. Pepper Beef
The Gypsy Kit

Chicken Yassa
Cazamance

Kimchi Fries with Beef Bulgogi
Chi'Lantro

Pancit Noodle Bowl
Be More Pacific

Polenta Cake with Poached Egg and Kale Pesto
Seedling Truck

Rockin' Shrimp Stratocaster
Kate's Southern Comfort

Royito's Fried Shrimp
Royito's Hot Sauce Streamer

Royito's Spicy Buttermilk Fried Chicken
Royito's Hot Sauce Streamer

Sweet Potato Gnocchi with Bolognese
Regal Ravioli

Watermelon Braised Pork
Kiss My Grits

Gluten-Free Vegetable Lasagna

Courtesy of Snap Pod

No noodles needed to make this classic homemade Italian dish.

Marinara Sauce:

1 cup extra-virgin olive oil

2 ounces garlic, peeled

8.6 ounces tomato paste

4 large cans whole tomatoes

1 cup basil

⅓ cup sea salt

1 tablespoon black pepper

Preparing the Marinara:

• Add the oil and the garlic to a large sauce pot and set over medium heat. As the oil heats up, the garlic will begin to toast. As the garlic starts to brown slightly, add the tomato paste and stir. This will start to melt the paste. Be careful not to burn the tomato paste.

• Next, add the entire can of tomatoes. Lower the heat and simmer the tomatoes for 20 minutes. Add the basil. Now, use the hand mixer or blender to puree the tomatoes until smooth. Adjust the seasoning to taste. Cool completely, using an ice bath if necessary.

Sautéed Mushrooms:

1 cup extra-virgin olive oil

2 pounds red onion, diced

10 pounds button mushrooms

6 tablespoons Herbes de Provence

2 tablespoons sea salt

2 tablespoons black pepper

Preparing the Mushrooms:

• In a large sauté pan over high heat, add oil and heat it until it almost smokes. Add onions, mushrooms and Herbes de Provence. Sauté by stirring the mushrooms to coat them with the oil. Add salt and black pepper. Cook until the liquid is released from the mushrooms, 10 to 12 minutes. Continue to cook until all the liquid is evaporated. The mushrooms will be cooked through. Adjust the seasoning. Remove the cooked mushrooms and drain them in a perforated pan. Place cooked mushrooms in fridge to cool completely.

Herbed Cheese:

10 cups part-skim ricotta cheese

8 whole eggs

4 tablespoons Italian herb blend

2 teaspoons sea salt

2 tablespoons black pepper

Preparing the Herbed Cheese:

• Drain the ricotta cheese of as much water/whey as

possible. Whip in the eggs and the spices with a whisk or spoon. Set aside until ready to assemble.

Lasagna:

1⅜ pounds roasted red bell peppers, peeled and diced

6 pounds eggplant, peeled, mandolin sliced thin

5 pounds summer squash, mandolin sliced thin

6 pounds zucchini, mandolin sliced thin

12 ounces Sautéed Mushrooms

1 tablespoon cooking spray

4 cups Marinara Sauce

10 cups Herbed Cheese

6 ounces Parmesan cheese

½ cup basil, as garnish

Preparing and Assembling the Lasagna:

• Place vegetables on baking sheets and sprinkle with salt. Bake for 15 minutes at 350°F. Drain the grilled vegetables on perforated pans overnight. Spray the bottom of a 200 pan (hotel pan or deep baking tray) with cooking spray.

• Place one layer of eggplant in pan. Spread one cup (8 ounces) of the Marinara Sauce evenly on top. Spread 3.3 cups of Herbed Cheese on top. Place a layer of the zucchini on top. Layer half of the amount of red peppers on top. Layer half of the amount of mushrooms on top. Place one layer of squash on top.

• Place one layer of eggplant on top. Spread 8 ounces of Marinara evenly on top.

Spread 3.3 cups of Herbed Cheese on top. Place one layer of zucchini on top. Layer remaining half of red peppers on top. Layer remaining half of mushrooms on top. Place one layer of squash on top.

• Place one layer of eggplant on top. Spread 8 ounces of Marinara evenly on top. Spread 3.3 cups of Herbed Cheese on top. Sprinkle 6 ounces of Parmesan cheese on top.

• Wrap entire pan with two layers of plastic wrap. Wrap entire pan with one layer of foil. Bake covered at 350°F for 45 minutes. Take pan out of oven and remove foil and plastic wrap. Bake uncovered at 300°F for an additional 30 minutes, turning the pan 180 degrees after 15 minutes to ensure an even bake.

Snap Pod, Martin Berson

Martin Berson has a history of restaurant ownership and management, so what about the trailer business sounded enticing to this chef entrepreneur? "By chance and coincidentally and as momentum grew in Austin for trailers, we thought we could stand out with our convenient, healthy and flavorful options. The lack of gluten-free and veggie-friendly options make Snap Pod unique amongst downtown eateries," shares Martin.

Their trailer is made from a shipping container and was previously a different trailer business. Martin's team outfitted the pod with hydraulic lifting doors, a clean paint job and the necessary coolers to run the business, and they were ready to serve.

The Bison Quinoa Hash is Martin's personal favorite item on the menu. It contains ground bison with quinoa, brown rice and veggies and is topped with cheese. But it's the Turkey Chili that is his bestseller.

Beef (or Lamb) with Prunes

Courtesy of The Flying Carpet

Don't forget to serve this meal with a French baguette to sop up the magical sauce.

1½ medium onions, finely chopped (any color onion)

5 medium garlic cloves, finely chopped

½ bunch cilantro, finely chopped

¼ teaspoon powdered ginger

½ teaspoon turmeric

5–10 stems of saffron

½ teaspoon cumin

sea salt and freshly ground black pepper, to taste

olive oil

2 pounds beef (rump is good for this rich dish, or if you prefer, you may use leg of lamb or lamb chops)

20 dried prunes

½ bunch Italian parsley, finely chopped

sesame seeds, to garnish

2–3 boiled eggs

• Sauté onions, garlic, cilantro and spices (ginger, turmeric, saffron, cumin, salt and pepper) with olive oil for approximately 5 minutes (or until onions are done giving off their juices).

• Add meat and sauté for another 5 to 10 minutes, being careful not to burn anything. Right before the meat and onion mixture seems like it is about to stick to the pan, add 1 cup water and cover to simmer for 1 to 1½ hours. Add water as necessary throughout the hour, just enough to keep a good amount of sauce at the bottom of the pan. Continue cooking until meat is tender. One technique to determine readiness is to take two forks and pull the meat off easily. If the meat is fighting you to stay together, it isn't ready yet.

• Add the prunes the last 10 minutes before the dish is done cooking. Serve with sesame seeds sprinkled on top of the beef, boiled eggs cut in half and French baguette.

Bourbon Braised Pork Shoulder with Cream Corn

Courtesy of Seedling Truck

Home chefs who are ready to try to take your cooking to a next level, this is a great dish to impress your guests. It also makes for a great family tradition meal during holidays.

1 bone-in pork shoulder

salt, to taste

pepper, to taste

4 cups bourbon

2 cups orange juice

½ cup brown sugar

2 shallots

fresh corn from 8 ears

2 tablespoons brandy

1 cup heavy cream

• Season pork shoulder with salt and pepper and put into a high-sided oven-safe vessel. In a bowl, mix bourbon, orange juice and brown sugar together and pour into vessel with pork. Cover with a lid or tin foil and roast in 300°F oven for 5 to 6 hours until fork tender.

• Sweat shallots in sauce pot over low heat for 3 minutes; add corn and cook for 4 minutes. The concept of "sweating" is to draw the water out of the ingredients to make them transparent without making anything crispy or changing color.

• Deglaze with brandy and add cream. If you are new to deglazing, the idea is to pour the brandy into the pan full of hot ingredients to get the flavorful bits off the bottom of the pan. You'll want to scrape the bottom to get all of the ingredients loose. This process takes less than a minute. Be careful: if you have too high of a heat, the alcohol will create a flame. You do not want a flame when deglazing. After deglazing, allow everything to simmer for 15 minutes.

• In a blender, puree ⅓ of the corn mixture then return it to the pot and stir to complete the creamed corn dish.

• Take pork out of oven and drain juices in small pot. Reduce the juices until the consistency is sticky enough to coat a spoon. Shred pork and baste with sauce. Serve over a bed of creamed corn.

Bufalo Bob's Shrimp Creole

Courtesy of Bufalo Bob's Chalupa Wagon

You probably have everything you need in your pantry to make this dish. Just grab some fresh shrimp on your way home.

¼ cup onion, chopped

¼ cup tomato, chopped

4 tablespoons olive oil

½ pound shrimp, peeled and deveined

1 teaspoon Creole seasoning

• Sauté onions and tomatoes in olive oil over medium heat for 15 to 20 minutes. Add shrimp and spices and sauté for another 8 to 10 minutes. Serve as entrée or over rice.

Bufalo Bob's Chalupa Wagon, R.J. Oliver

"The chalupa is the second cousin to the taco. It is my mission to bring the chalupa to a place of honor in the culinary hierarchy," says R.J. "Bufalo Bob" Oliver through his mustache.

"As my wife and I were getting older, we began to realize what we eat affects our lives. I needed to start watching my health, and her diet called to remove gluten and soy. I needed to make a radical change in my diet. My doctor wanted to give me all sorts of drugs, but I'm averse to taking medication. So what I did was, I looked at it as a challenge to change my diet in a way that was better for me. Finding the chalupa and turning it into a healthy thing made it a fun thing to do. The first thing I did was find a low-fat tostada. Once you take the lard out of it, a chalupa is actually healthy for you. I replace the lard with olive oil and have dropped my cholesterol substantially," shares Bufalo Bob.

Bufalo Bob is passionate about bringing traditional Mexican street food and western flavors to a new level in gourmet street food. With the art of the chalupa, he uses local products to top his tostadas. He was recently an Austin ambassador for Jamie Oliver's food revolution foundation. His Cordoba chalupa won the mayor's fitness challenge, A Taste of Health, during the Austin chef showdown. The Cordoba is topped with hummus, flaxseed, bison, onions, spinach, tomatoes and Parmesan cheese.

The Armadillo is Bufalo Bob's bestseller. It is topped with refried beans, rice, a Monterey jack and Colby jack cheese mixture, bison, onions, lettuce and tomatoes all on a gluten-free tostada. You might try his Texas Hummus, which is made of things a cowboy might find available: beer, pinto beans, peanut butter and a good shot of chipotle seasoning.

The beautiful painting on the back of his trailer features local Austin songwriters and musicians. At least one of the featured artists, Marcia Ball, has come to have a chalupa. "I've lived in Austin for over thirty years. I play music. To me, it's the music scene that makes Austin what it is," shares Bufalo Bob.

Butternut Squash Ravioli with Fontina Cheese Veloute

Courtesy of Regal Ravioli

The perfect nurturing and nourishing dish to ring in the fall flavors.

Filling:

- 2 medium butternut squash, split and roasted skin side down at 375°F for 1¼ hours, deseeded, scooped and pureed in food processor
- 1 small to medium yellow onion, chopped, sautéed until caramelized and pureed with squash
- 2 poblano peppers roasted, deseeded, skin peeled and chopped
- ⅓ of whole nutmeg seed, freshly grated
- salt, to taste
- white pepper, to taste

• Combine above ingredients and stuff dollops in between sheets of your favorite fresh pasta recipe. Remember to wet edges so the pasta sticks together where you want it to stick together and use plenty of flour to keep everything else from sticking together. Use a ravioli mold or a sturdy wine glass to cut the ravioli out. Boil ravioli in water until desired doneness, approximately 8 to 11 minutes. Serve with Veloute Sauce.

Veloute Sauce:

- ¼ medium red onion, minced
- 4 tablespoons butter
- 4 tablespoons flour
- 2 cups vegetable stock
- 1 cup heavy cream
- ⅓ cup grated Parmesan cheese
- ½ cup grated fontina cheese
- salt and white pepper to taste

• Sauté onion in butter until soft; add flour. Make a light roux, slowly adding vegetable stock, heavy cream, Parmesan and fontina a little at a time, stirring continuously. Season with salt and pepper.

Dr. Pepper Beef

Courtesy of The Gypsy Kit

"I met my husband in San Diego, and he took me on a date to eat a California Burrito. It was a large flour tortilla stuffed with crispy French fries, carne esada and spicy sour cream. When he moved to Texas about a year later, he was desperately craving a California Burrito, so I put my own Texas spin on it and came up with my version: Dr. Pepper Beef, Seasoned French Fries, Black Bean and Corn Relish, Srirachi Mayo and Lime Sour Cream," says Tagan Couch.

2 pounds skirt steak, cleaned and trimmed

1 cup sweet chili sauce

1 (12-ounce) can Dr. Pepper

• Combine all ingredients in Crock-Pot and cover for 6 hours on low. Meat will shred and the sauce will reduce and become like a BBQ sauce. Serve on tortillas for tacos or bread with blue cheese coleslaw for an awesome sandwich.

Chicken Yassa

Courtesy of Cazamance

The pride of Senegal. If you want to eat this for dinner, put it in the fridge in the morning to marinate all day. Yassa is a unique African dish that originates from Cazamance. Everything needed to make the dish comes from Senegal. Yassa was originally made with a certain fish from the nearest river and the white long-grain rice grown there. The dish became famous for being so healthy and easy to make and became a staple in many households. Because chicken is a favorite thing to serve guests, it is popular to replace the fish with chicken for special occasions.
Yield: 4 servings.

2 boneless, skinless chicken breasts, or enough for 8 tenders

½ cup grape seed oil (¼ cup to cook chicken and ¼ cup in marinade)

2 large Spanish onions, julienned

2 large red bell peppers, julienned

3 regular or 2 large poblano pepers, julienned

1 cup sliced green olives

5 cloves garlic chopped finely

1 tablespoon Dijon mustard

1 tablespoon lemon pepper

salt to taste

½ teaspoon cayenne pepper

½ cup water

2 cups white basmati rice, cooked

Option: Replace chicken with 4 portobello mushrooms to make this a vegetarian dish.

• Start by cutting the raw chicken breasts into medium-sized strips like tenders. You may substitute dark meat if you prefer. In a large mixing bowl, pour ¼ cup grape seed oil over the chicken. Add onions, red bell peppers, poblanos, green olives and garlic. Add all of the spices: Dijon, lemon pepper, salt and cayenne. Mix ingredients really well until spices are distributed evenly. Let this marinate for at least half an hour.

• When you are ready to begin cooking, heat ¼ cup grape seed oil in a deep skillet over medium heat. After a few minutes, when the oil is really hot, put only the chicken in to brown, taking care to make sure no onions or other ingredients stuck to the chicken. Cook tender strips for about 3 minutes on each side.

• Add the vegetable mix to the chicken cooking in the skillet and let it simmer about 5 to 10 minutes until the onions become clear in color. Continue simmering.

• Add ½ cup of water in the mixing bowl and scrape the sides of the mixing bowl to take the remaining seasoning and stir into the water. Add the seasoned water to the cooking chicken and vegetable mix; cover and let it simmer for about 20 minutes.

• Serve yassa on top of a bed of cooked white rice.

• With leftovers, Iba likes to serve the yassa as a wrap with spinach and feta in a tortilla. Another option he likes is to make a quesadilla with

the yassa and pepper jack cheese. Serve quesadillas with his Sour Cream Sriracha Sauce (see page 63).

Vegetarian option: Portobello mushrooms cook faster than chicken. Leave them whole and marinate like above. Cook them separately from the mix on a different skillet

with a tablespoon of oil (they will also have juices from the marinade on them). Sear them for one minute on each side and then add to the completed sauce mixture.

Cazamance, Iba Thiam

Iba Thiam was born in a Muslim home in West Central Africa. Breakfast was his favorite meal. As a child, all eight children in his family sat at the kitchen table together and ate leftovers from the night before—stuffed cream cheese, toast and coffee—before walking with thirty of the neighborhood kids to school. He says, "Breakfast was my favorite meal growing up. I loved it so much that it inspired me to become who I am today."

In his home in Senegal, each household had two main roles: the women cooked and the men cleaned. He always wanted to be one of those men, not because of any particular fascination with the workings of keeping a household clean and tidy but because after the kids went to school, the men were the only ones left in the house. "I wanted to be alone in the house with all those leftovers from breakfast."

"When I think about it now, I see that what I wanted to do as a child is what I am doing now as an adult. I take care of people with my food. Those men from my childhood taught me hospitality. I am the first male cook in my family," he says.

While the men taught Iba hospitality, his grandmother Tara taught him a love for cooking. Everyone was glad to get up very early in the morning because they knew Tara's cooking would be ready for them on the table. Her kitchen was built outside of her house like the traditional families still have in Africa.

Eventually, Iba made his way to France, New York and then Austin, where he started the Cazamance food trailer as a nod to the menu from his heritage. His passion for serving people food that looks, smells and tastes good keeps patrons coming back meal after meal.

Kimchi Fries with Beef Bulgogi

Courtesy of Chi'Lantro

This is the most popular dish from one of Austin's favorite food trucks.
Yield: 4 servings.

Bulgogi:

1 small onion, minced

3 garlic cloves, minced

1 tablespoon fresh ginger, minced

½ cup soy sauce

2 tablespoons sugar

2 tablespoons distilled white vinegar

1 teaspoon toasted sesame oil

1 pound boneless rib-eye steak, cut into 3-inch slices

1 tablespoon vegetable oil

Toppings:

½ cup sugar

¼ cup distilled white vinegar

2 tablespoons Korean chile paste

2 tablespoons soy sauce

1 cup kimchi

½ cup mayonnaise

3 tablespoons Sriracha, plus more for serving

1 pound hot French fries

shredded cheddar, chopped white onion, toasted sesame seeds and cilantro for serving

- First, make the bulgogi. In a resealable plastic bag, combine the onion, garlic, ginger, soy sauce, sugar, vinegar and sesame oil. Add the rib-eye and toss to coat. Seal the bag and refrigerate overnight.

- Drain the meat, pick off the solids and pat dry. In a large skillet, heat the vegetable oil until smoking. Add the meat and cook over high heat, turning once, until lightly browned, 4 minutes. Transfer the meat to a plate and keep warm. Rinse out the skillet and wipe dry.

- Next, prepare the toppings. In a medium bowl, combine the sugar, vinegar, chile paste and soy sauce. Add the kimchi and toss to coat. Heat the skillet until very hot. Add the kimchi and cook over high heat until the liquid is thickened and glossy and the kimchi is browned in spots, about 5 minutes.

- In a small bowl, whisk the mayonnaise with the Sriracha.

- Scatter the French fries on a platter and top with the bulgogi and kimchi. Drizzle with some of the Sriracha mayonnaise and sprinkle with cheddar, onion, sesame seeds and cilantro. Serve with additional Sriracha.

Chi'Lantro, Jae Kim

"I always had passion in the food industry. I started a coffee shop when I was twenty-one and moved on to working in the seafood industry for two years. I wanted to start a brick and mortar but didn't have enough capital to start. One day, I woke up, prayed and said I'm just going to do this and see what happens. Three months later, I opened a food truck."

Jae Kim was born in Seoul, Korea, Oppan Gangnam style. He moved to the States when he was eleven and was raised in Orange County, California. Making his way to Texas because of love, he began his food truck empire in Austin in February 2010. Known for the bestselling Kimchi Fries, this menu item was born in Austin and is the foundation of Chi'Lantro's success. Voted *Food and Wine*'s staff favorite in May 2012, Chi'Lantro continues to receive accolades and awards from foodie notables. Jae's tacos and fries have gotten nods from Tom Colicchio, Aaron Sanchez and Roger Mooking. If you ask Jae who his least expected customers are, he'll tell you he is surprised that even kids love his Kimchi Fries. "Kids bring their parents because they were craving Chi'Lantro. It's pretty awesome," says Jae.

Pancit Noodle Bowl

Courtesy of Be More Pacific

This is a yummy recipe for rice noodles and fresh vegetables.

½ bag thin rice noodles, uncooked

½ pound green cabbage, shredded

1 carrot, shredded (about 4 ounces)

part of a yellow onion, julienned (about 2 ounces)

½ stalk of celery, sliced (about 2 ounces)

3–4 ounces vegetable bouillon (mixed with water)

1 tablespoon oyster sauce

• Boil rice noodles for about 1 minute. Strain and run under cool water until the noodles have cooled down. Cut noodles on a chopping board so they are about 6 to 8 inches in length. Set aside.

• Chop all vegetables and set aside in a bowl. Preferably using a wok, first sauté all the vegetables until they are about halfway cooked, a few minutes. Add the noodles, vegetable bouillon and oyster sauce to taste, making sure it is thoroughly mixed. Add any cooked protein you prefer (chicken, shrimp, beef, etc.). Toss everything together and serve in bowls.

Polenta Cake with Poached Egg and Kale Pesto

Courtesy of Seedling Truck

1 quart whole milk

1 cup polenta or cornmeal

1 teaspoon kosher salt

¼ teaspoon cracked black pepper

3 tablespoons unsalted butter

1 bunch kale (cleaned and torn into pieces)

2 cloves garlic

⅔ cup olive oil

1 tablespoon white vinegar

4 eggs

4 tablespoons fresh goat chevre

For the Polenta:

• In medium pot over medium heat, warm up milk until just barely simmering. Slowly add in polenta while stirring. Keep stirring for 8 to 10 minutes. As mixture begins to thicken, make sure it does not stick to bottom of the pot and burn.

• Take pot off heat and add salt and pepper and butter, allowing the butter to melt into polenta. Pour polenta into a rectangular baking dish so it is at least ¾ of an inch deep all around. Refrigerate until ready for use.

For the Pesto:

• In a food processor, combine kale and peeled garlic cloves. Pulse and slowly start to add olive oil in a stream until mixture starts to make a paste. Set aside.

For the Egg:

• Warm 8 cups water in sauce pot over medium heat. Once water is just barely simmering, add the vinegar. Turn the heat down slightly and crack eggs into water. Allow egg to poach for 4 to 5 minutes until the whites have set and the egg can be scooped out of the water.

How to Assemble:

• Cut polenta with a round cookie cutter to make the cakes. Sear the polenta cakes in a hot, nonstick pan with 1 tablespoon of olive oil until brown and crispy on the outside, a few minutes depending on heat. Top the cake with poached egg and pesto. Sprinkle with goat cheese.

Seedling Truck, Dan and Kristen Stacy

After four years of owning a successful catering business, Dan and Kristen Stacy from the Royal Fig decided to open a food trailer. "It is a creative outlet from our catering business and gives us a chance to play around with new menu items," shares chef Dan. The trailer space itself is a far cry from the country club and fine dining kitchens Dan had previously worked in, but the food is not. The Polenta Cake with Poached Egg and Kale Pesto is their most popular dish, and although their menu rotates, this is one item that cannot be removed. "Our food is unique and changes nearly every day. We also use mostly local products, so when you eat at Seedling, you are supporting many local farmers," Dan explains.

The concept is an extension of the food philosophy they have for their catering operation. It took the couple about five months to open the truck. Dan jokes, "We have a 1979 Chevy step van (it's older than I am). We bought it in Dallas and totally gutted it and outfitted it with the equipment we needed." The Seedling Truck is available for special events and can be seen roaming the wedding scene.

Kate's Southern Comfort, Kate Bellinger

By the time Kate came of age, she had eaten her last East Texas casserole and began learning how to cook much spicier cuisine in Louisiana. After working at different restaurants, she decided to give her food trailer concept a go. Her menu is based around savory Louisiana fried pies. The pies are "affordable for me to make, affordable for anyone to eat and they are good grab-and-go food that you can take on a picnic, down to the [Barton] Springs or sit at the trailer," Kate says.

The Nak.i.tish has a spicy, peppery pork filling, while the Humble Pie is filled with mustard greens, collard greens and sweet potato. The Bleudan was originally an honest mistake in the kitchen but has turned out to be one of her bestsellers. It contains boudin sausage and bleu cheese. When the Hatch Green Chile, Chicken and Cheese fried pie is on special, her fans can't wait to come out for a fried pie and hope for a pot of gumbo.

Rockin' Shrimp Stratocaster

Courtesy of Kate's Southern Comfort

Serve with toasty garlic bread and a nice chilled white wine. Don't forget the white wine.

¼ cup Zatarain's crab boil

2 pounds Texas gulf shrimp (medium to large)

½ cup butter

1 tablespoon chopped garlic

1 cup medium red onion, chopped

1 pound crimini mushrooms, sliced

1 pound sugar snap peas

1 cup green onion, finely diced

1 quart half and half

1 lemon

Tabasco, salt and pepper to taste

8 ounces good Parmesan or asiago cheese or both

24 ounces good pasta (we like linguini, and spinach is really good)

• Heat a large pot of water with the crab boil and bring to a fast boil. Add cold shrimp and cook until al dente, a few minutes. Remove shrimp and save the water. Peel the shrimp and set aside.

• Melt butter in large sauté pan and add garlic, red onions and mushrooms. Sauté on medium-low heat, about 10 minutes or until tender. Add sugar snap peas and green onions and cook for another 4 minutes. Set the pan of veggies aside with the shrimp.

• Bring shrimp boil water back to a boil and cook the pasta in it. While the noodles are cooking, heat the half and half, juice and zest from the lemon and seasonings (Tabasco, salt and pepper to taste). Bring to a slow simmer, watching that it does not scorch. Once thickened, add the shrimp and veggie mixture while the pasta is draining.

• Spoon pasta into bowls and portion the sauce and shrimp. Top with a sprinkle of cheese and a few more drops of hot sauce.

Royito's Fried Shrimp

Courtesy of Royito's Hot Sauce Streamer

Dip these hot and spicy shrimp in Royito's hot sauce.

1 pound shrimp, peeled and deveined

1½ cups of Royito's, reserving ½ cup

1 quart canola oil

2 eggs

1 cup self-rising flour

2 teaspoons salt

1 teaspoon pepper

1 teaspoon paprika

1 teaspoon garlic powder

• In a plastic bag or bowl, mix together shrimp and one cup of Royito's and let marinate in the refrigerator for 1 to 2 hours. In a large pot, preheat canola oil to 375°F.

• In a bowl, whisk together eggs and ½ cup of Royito's. In a separate dish, mix together flour, salt, pepper, paprika and garlic powder. Dip each individual shrimp in the egg mixture followed by the flour mixture and then directly into the hot oil, cooking 1 to 2 minutes on each side until they are golden brown on the outside. Make sure not to crowd the pot with too many shrimp at once.

• Once cooked through, place the shrimp on a plate lined with paper towel to collect the excess cooking oil.

Royito's Hot Sauce Streamer, Roy Spence

Austinite Roy Spence was walking Miss Ellie, his Labrador, down South Congress one morning when he walked by a food trailer court. That's when it hit him. He had a realization that food trailers are part of a larger movement to revitalize small business in America. It was that moment on an early morning in downtown Austin that Roy decided he was going to marry his passion for inspiring business owners to start their own businesses with his own trailer food concept: all-natural hot sauce.

Having been a founding partner at the distinguished GSD&M advertising agency for over forty years in Austin, Roy may seem like an unusual candidate to participate in the trailer food world. Although from an advertising standpoint he has represented such restaurants as Chili's, Macaroni Grill, On the Border and many more corporate chains, Roy's experience with the food industry stops there and starts in his own kitchen. "I handmade tens of thousands of jars of hot sauce and sent them to restaurant owners and friends, and everyone kept asking, 'When can we buy this?' I finally decided I was cheating the world out of the opportunity to have a big dose of spice in their life," Roy says with a big smile on his face.

Over fifteen years in the making, Roy finally perfected his hot sauce and put it in jars to be sold across the country. Named Royito's, since that is what his dad used to call him, the trailer stands for more than just good salsa. The "don't do mild" tagline is something he learned from his father and is part of the Royito's mission to not do mild in life or in salsa. "Dad taught me three things: be kind to everyone you meet, keep it simple and don't do mild," shares Roy.

Passing the tradition down to his son, Shay Spence is now using Royito's hot sauce as a way to explore his culinary interests and is currently the head chef at his father's hot sauce company.

Royito's Spicy Buttermilk Fried Chicken

Courtesy of Royito's Hot Sauce Streamer

This dish will become a new Sunday family meal favorite in your household.

1 whole chicken, cut into 10 pieces

3 cups buttermilk

1 jar (2 cups) Royito's

canola oil for frying

3 eggs

2 cups self-rising flour

2 teaspoons pepper

1 tablespoon salt

1 teaspoon paprika

2 teaspoons garlic powder

1 teaspoon cayenne pepper

• Place chicken in a casserole dish or resealable plastic bag. Mix together buttermilk with one cup of Royito's, pour over the chicken and let marinate for at least two hours or up to twenty-four hours.

• Fill a deep pan up to halfway full with canola oil; heat to 350°F. In a bowl, mix together 3 eggs with one cup of Royito's.

• In a separate dish, mix together self-rising flour, pepper, salt, paprika, garlic powder and cayenne. Dip each individual chicken piece in the egg mixture followed by the flour mixture and then directly into the hot oil. Cook 8 to 10 minutes for light meat and 13 to 15 minutes for dark meat. Remove from fryer onto baking sheet lined with paper towel to collect excess grease.

Sweet Potato Gnocchi with Bolognese

Courtesy of Regal Ravioli

Make this homemade gnocchi a special tradition with your family.

Gnocchi:

2 pounds potatoes (2 parts sweet, 1 part white baking)

kosher salt, to taste

ground white pepper, to taste

¼ cup shredded Romano cheese

½ nutmeg seed, freshly grated

2 eggs, 1 yolk

unbleached all-purpose flour (as needed)

• Peel and boil potatoes until a fork inserts easily (do not overcook or potato will absorb too much water). Run potato through ricer (food mill) directly onto stainless-steel table or butcher block. Heavily salt and pepper the potato on table. Using two bench scrapers, mix in cheese, nutmeg and eggs, then begin to add flour, sprinkling in a little at a time. Continue kneading flour into dough until dough ball stiffens and becomes less sticky. Cut sections of dough ball and roll into ropes (continue to flour the table as you work). Cut the ropes into bite-size pieces with the bench scraper. You can freeze the gnocchi or boil it in water right away. Gnocchi are done cooking when they all float, approximately 5 minutes. Serve with Bolognese Sauce.

Bolognese Sauce:

1 pound ground beef

½ pound ground pork (shoulder if possible)

salt and pepper to taste

¼ pound finely chopped prosciutto

¼ cup olive oil

1 onion, minced

3 celery stalks, minced

2 carrots, minced

6 garlic cloves, minced

1 teaspoon crushed red pepper

5 ounces dry red wine

¼ cup chopped parsley

60 ounces tomato puree

1 cup chicken stock

• Spread out ground beef and pork on a baking sheet. Season heavily with salt and pepper. Bake in oven at 425°F for about 20 minutes to brown the meat. Do not drain. Set meat aside to cool.

• In a 6-quart stock pot, sauté prosciutto in olive oil until evenly browned, then add the onion, celery, carrots, garlic and crushed red pepper. sauté on low-medium heat until the moisture has been removed from the veggies. Add red wine and cook until veggies absorb the liquid. Add parsley, tomato puree and chicken stock. Bring sauce to a boil. Chop the cooked ground meat and add to hot sauce, along with all the fat and drippings in the pan. Reduce to a simmer and cook 1¾ hours. Salt and pepper to taste.

Regal Ravioli, Zach Adams

Dishwasher, line cook, pizza cook, waiter, bartender, bar manager, dining room manager, general manager, facilities manager for six unique restaurant concepts in Northern Virginia, bartender in Austin…Regal Ravioli. The progression from washing dishes to owning his own food trailer was years of hard work for Zach Adams. "I felt compelled to work for myself. I combined all of the skills I had learned working in the industry over the last fifteen years with a tiny budget and was left with Regal Ravioli," shares Zach.

"My mom is full-blooded Sicilian and never cooks Italian food, or at least never did when I was living in her house. She prefers to cook Asian instead and is a very good sushi maker. What's up with that?" Zach laughs about his heritage. Nevertheless, Regal Ravioli offers honest, handmade raviolis and pastas of restaurant quality at a food trailer. Cheese Ravioli are the most popular item on the menu: four enormous oval ravioli stuffed with ricotta, mozzarella and Romano cheeses with fresh basil, lemon zest and nutmeg. Customers can pair the ravioli with tomato marinara, Bolognese, pecan pesto or fontina cheese veloute sauce. The Sweet Potato Gnocchi with Bolognese is Zach's personal favorite: soft and chewy bite-sized sweet potato and flour dumplings topped with a tomato-based sauce made from prosciutto, ground beef and pork.

"Originally, my trailer hauled motorcycles. It was renovated to serve as a food trailer two owners previous. I renovated again after I purchased it from a fellow running a business called the Big Tex Express. The side of the trailer had a painted twenty-foot Texas flag set aflame," Zach shares about his food trailer, which is now tempered a mustard yellow.

Watermelon Braised Pork

Courtesy of Kiss My Grits

"I first discovered this unique combination by accident, and as soon as it came to me, I couldn't believe I'd never thought of it before. I'd bought the pork shoulder and the watermelon for a Fourth of July cookout that had not transpired. A few days later, I discovered them in my fridge and not much else. I'd recently found a taco truck that served the most sublime version of Al Pastor I'd ever tried, and re-creating it at home had been on my mind a lot. When the idea to replace the pineapple with watermelon came to me, I realized I was possibly onto something great. I could not have been more surprised, or satisfied, with the finished product. The sugary cubes of melon melted into the pork stew in such a way as to become almost unidentifiably mellow and savory. I recommend using this to make sandwiches, tacos, empanadas, pizzas, burritos, baked potatoes, anything really where you want the succulent addition of slowly braised, spiced pork," says Christopher Crowley.
Yield: 15 (4-ounce) sandwiches or 30 (2-ounce) tacos.

6 pounds pork shoulder, medium diced

1 cup all-purpose flour

¼ cup canola oil

¼ cup bacon, diced small

3 white onions, minced

3 tablespoons garlic, minced

2 tablespoons salt

1 tablespoon oregano

1 tablespoon cumin

¾ cup apple cider vinegar

1 small watermelon, seeded and diced

2 chipotle peppers, canned

2 tablespoons adobo sauce

¾ cup ancho powder

• In a metal bowl, toss diced pork shoulder with flour. Using a mesh strainer or colander, sift off excess flour and discard.

• In a large stock pot, heat canola oil. Over medium heat, add diced bacon and stir until bacon is fully cooked and crisp, about 8 minutes. Remove bacon from oil with a slotted spoon and place on a paper towel. Set aside.

• In the same pot, add floured pork chunks in small batches and sear on all sides. Remove to a paper towel and set aside. Repeat until all pork is cooked.

• In the same pot, add onion and sauté until onion is nicely caramelized, about 5 minutes. Add garlic and sauté until aromatic. Add the salt, oregano and cumin. Stir until aromatic.

• Deglaze the pan with vinegar, scraping up all the brown bits stuck to the bottom of the pan. Add the watermelon, chipotle, adobo sauce and ancho powder. Bring to a boil and lower to a simmer. Add the cubed pork and bacon back to the pot carefully. Stir well and allow to simmer until pork shreds easily, about an hour. Stir frequently, paying special attention to the bottom of the pan.

Kiss My Grits, Christopher Crowley

Christopher Crowley had been an executive chef, among other swanky kitchen positions, before embarking on his food trailer business. With a name like Kiss My Grits, it's only appropriate that the Shrimp and Grits is his favorite dish. "I've been preaching the gospel of shrimp and grits since I moved here, so if you're still unconverted, you should definitely come see us," says Christopher. Six jumbo Gulf shrimp sautéed with wild mushrooms, bacon and fresh herbs in a white wine cream sauce served over Anson Mills yellow quick grits is just one example of the neoclassic southern dishes served out of the trailer.

Originally from Cadaretta, Mississippi, Christopher's main sources of inspiration come from his family tree. "My menu was inspired by my culinary heroes: Chef Bill Neal, my mother, Shirley Ann, and my grandmothers, Elma Orene and Ola Mae," shares Christopher.

"In the short time I've been open, the word of mouth has really spread. I've had several people drive from Georgetown and Houston to try us just on a recommendation. The owner of a local soul food restaurant came in with his family just before close one day and bought everything I had left," says the chef.

Tips from the Trailers: Do You Have What It Takes to Run a Food Truck?

I f you're thinking about starting your own food trailer business, the modern-day food truck entrepreneurs have some advice for you. I asked them to share some tips for new vendors. My question to them: What do you wish someone had told you before you started? They responded:

Jae Kim, Chi'Lantro: "Dream big. Be persistent. Customers are our bosses; make sure to take care of them and give them what they want."

Sam Rhodes, SoCo to Go: "It's *hot* out there! The weather definitely contributes to your dine-in business, whether it be cold or hot (mostly hot) or rainy…be prepared for slower times. Our delivery option definitely gives us the best of both worlds and helps offset slower dining times. Things in trailers break, so learn to be handy or have a good handyman on call. Once you can figure things out, most repairs can be made pretty easily."

Julia Hungerford, Schmaltz: "I am a new vendor and I am learning every day. It's a pretty burly job. It's super hot (108 daily, even with air conditioning in the summer), for one thing. I would recommend using different equipment or learning new techniques to keep the heat down."

Rena Willis, MamboBerry: "1) Everything that can possibly go wrong will. Twice. 2) It's not easier than opening a restaurant; it's more difficult in many ways. You have to play every single role/ position. You're the order taker, server, chef, call taker, purchaser, manager, accountant, marketing and advertising department, etc. You handle absolutely everything. And since it is such a small business, many times, there is no one there to help in times of chaos. 3) Do it because you're passionate about it, not for the money. It's a very difficult business and won't make you rich quick, if ever. But if you're passionate about food and your concept, it's an amazing opportunity to turn your dream into a reality."

Mark Pascual, Be More Pacific: "Make sure that you are not only clean but that your kitchen looks clean. Always taste your food. Make friends with other trailers."

Levi Smith, Woodpile BBQ: "If you're in Texas, install the biggest air conditioner you have space for or can afford. There's never enough counter space in a trailer. Give yourself an hour buffer every day for something to go wrong. Expect the unexpected."

Lara Enzor, Bow Wow Chow: "Budget twice as much money and twice as much time as you think it will take to get started. Use your ninja skills to be nimble and flexible and roll gracefully with the speed bumps. Food trucks are about passion and love for your product and customers—not about getting rich."

Tagan Couch, The Gypsy Kit: "July and August are the worst months for food trailers in Austin. Make sure you have access to plenty of electricity in your trailer. 'Without struggle, there is no progress!'—this is the tattoo I got right before taking on this endeavor. I have to look in the mirror every day to remind myself that although it is tough work and oftentimes discouraging, we will make a name for ourselves and spread our love of food."

Richard Kreuzburg, ChocoSutra: "1) It's not as hard as you might expect! 2) The Health Department is your friend. 3) Make sure you love what you're doing; on slow days, it'll make it worth it."

Candy Silva, Colibri Cuisine: "Be ready to put all your time and energy to the business; work long and hard."

Rishi Dhir, Conscious Cravings: "I would say to make sure you are really passionate about the business because it's a ton of work and is a lot tougher than you might think. I would also say that you must be patient with growth. Also, I think people underestimate how much the weather can affect business. Weather forecasts are a big part of how we staff for the following week."

Chris Howell, The Fat Cactus: "1) It's going to take longer than you think (getting open, making a profit, selling franchises, retiring a multimillionaire) 2) Be open when you say you are; you never know who might come when, and it's no fun getting called out in Yelp, blogs or big-time magazines. 3) Enjoy and appreciate your successes because they are hard-fought and you earned it."

R.J. Oliver, Bufalo Bob's Chalupa Wagon: "You have to have perseverance, that's the number one thing. You need a good idea, something that stands out and is a little bit different. You need to be consistent with your hours—be open when you say you're going to be open."

India Moore, Lovebaked (San Marcos): "Get your gray water disposal worked out before you begin. This can be a major hassle if you don't have a solution. Your workspace will be smaller than you anticipate once you begin. Spend a lot of time organizing your trailer in regard to space. It's going to be hot in there in the summer. If you can afford it and the logistics of your trailer allow it, spring for a second AC."

Celena McGuill, Lovebaked (San Marcos): "Great—not good—customer service should always be a top priority. Never compromise quality to save time and money. Quality is KING. Keep consistent food trailer hours. Your customers need to know they can rely on your hours or they will stop frequenting your business. I have seen many food trailers with inconsistent hours/days, etc., and so many customers get upset because they stop in to eat only to find their favorite food trailer is not open."

Bruce Bryson, The Caboose (San Marcos): "Be prepared for downtime you can't control."

Fred Varela, The Patty Wagon (San Marcos): "Use fresh products, be consistent and prepare meals as you would eat them."

Mark Jakobsen, The Big Kahuna (San Marcos): "Do thorough research, find a good location and try to offer food that no one else has. Make learning promotion techniques a priority."

Monica Coggin, How Sweet It Is: "1) Offer items on your menu that you personally love. Selling stuff you like is so much easier than stuff you don't. 2) Don't list your personal cellphone on your business cards… those suckers hang out in the universe for a long time. (I still get calls.) 3) Reward your regulars. Nothing is more valuable than word of mouth advertising."

Kara Jordan, Blenders and Bowls: "Keep it simple! When we first started, we thought we could have this big and lavish menu, but once we got in our truck, we soon realized that it was just not possible in such a small space. When starting a food truck, you have to stay in the food truck mindset. You're not opening a huge restaurant—it's a truck. Simplify and your life will be easier."

Erin Downing, Blenders and Bowls: "Get a handyman around if you aren't one. Budget higher than expected. Try anything/location at least once!"

Daniel Oliveira, Cow Bell's: "1) Do your research on everything. I tried to look up and read anything I could get my hands on regarding the food trailer game. 2) Give everything a test drive before the opening day. Cook off a few meals and get some reps before the big dance. 3) Be prepared to work long days. My food trailer is like my baby, and I want to give my baby my undivided attention. Be there all the time so you can figure out when you're busy and when you're not. This will make writing the schedule easier and more efficient. One thing I didn't realize is how much of a team effort it was and how many different players are involved in the creation of our food trailer. Sign guys, managers at the local markets, welder, trailer guys, an artist who designed our logo, kitchen equipment guys, photo copy guy, web designer, friends, family and many more. It was a great experience in the start-up phase getting to know so many different, skilled professionals."

Kesten Broughton, Sun Farm Kitchen: "Go in with a partner. Have great signage. Pick the right location."

Christopher Crowley, Kiss My Grits: "Restaurant experience alone is not enough. Work in a high-volume trailer if possible for at least six months. The trailer operators I know are a very helpful, tightknit group. Support them, and don't be too proud to ask questions."

Chuck Watkins, Snarky's Moo Bawk Oink: "You need restaurant experience. It is actually harder in some ways to manage day-to-day operations in a trailer setting. Problem solving and logistics are necessary skills. Somebody that cooks at home will find it hard to maintain quality/consistency in a commercial setting."

Ray Gonzalez, WhaTaTaco: "1) It's not going to be easy and be patient. 2) Do a lot of research on locations before starting your project. 3) Try always to give something extra plus a smile to the customers. I wish someone would have told me how difficult it is to get through the inspection and how much time and policies you need to follow."

Lee Krasner, Dock and Roll Diner: "I would say keep your head down, work hard, create a menu you believe in with food you are passionate about and give your customers a great experience. Most importantly, don't get down on yourself because it will most likely be the hardest thing you have ever done. Be in it for the right reasons may be a good piece of advice too, as I would say there are multiple people out there who want to get into the trailer business only to make money quickly, which is going to be very hard to do."

Tova Ng, Fresh Off the Truck: "1) Market well. 2) Have a good mechanic. 3) It gets hot in Austin, so make sure you have some way to stay hydrated and cool inside the trailers and have good help."

Eric Regan, Hey!…You Gonna Eat or What?: "1) Expect to work harder than you've ever worked. 2) Explore food that excites you and dishes you can be proud of serving. Take pride in what you're doing. 3.)Consider ways to do more with less ingredients. Space constraints will hamper you if you have a truck full of ingredients that are used for a single dish."

Lee Dockery, Ice Cream Social: "One thing we tell new vendors is to work closely with the Health Department because there's a *lot* to learn and a lot of rules. Also, just perfect the hell out of your recipes and worry about the details once you get open. Baptism by fire. Just jump in and learn as you go. As long as you're confident in your product, everything else will fall into place. Over time, that is."

Scott Angle, Honky Tonk Hot Dogs: "Do your homework! Pick a good location and don't expect to set the world on fire your first year…it takes time to build a business."

Willy Pearce, Way South Philly: "1) Location is essential. 2) Social media is your best friend! 3) Listen to your customers. They will tell you how to succeed. 4) Cook what you're passionate about."

Josie Paredes, La Fantabulous: "I wish someone would have told me about all the regulations and permits."

Angela Stringer, Tenderland: "1) Understand that it is very rewarding and a lot of work. 2) Talk to other trailer owners prior to starting your business. 3) Talk to the local city Health Department before you purchase or design your trailer—it'll save you lots of money and time. Wish somebody would have told me it'll be 120-plus on some days inside our trailer during the hot summer months in Austin."

Corey Sorenson, Cow Tipping Creamery: "Question local laws for parking and registration. You want to keep mindful of the area you are in when it comes to being mobile. Make sure you have the right permits for your area. You don't want to have a permit for the wrong county. Make sure you have easy access to fresh water and have a place to dump gray water."

Jason Umlas, Lucky J's Chicken & Waffles: "Your ego is not always your amigo. If your business plan doesn't make sense on paper, it's not going to make cents on the street."

Martin Berson, Snap Pod: "Find your niche, find a location that you are unlikely to be displaced from and engage your customers in all social media channels and in store to find out their preferences."

Zach Adams, Regal Ravioli: "Have the business be as truly mobile as possible. Do not do it by yourself unless you are of the most hardened stock. Plan ahead and shop around for things like insurance, credit card processing, commissary, etc."

Dan Stacy, Seedling Truck: "1) Talk to other vendors about the challenges and day-to-day operations of a trailer. 2) Read the weather forecast every day. 3) Be nice to your food trailer neighbors."

Nic Patrizi, The Jalopy: "Have passion for what you are setting out to do; it will show in your product. Remember your roots and use them to your advantage. Don't be too overzealous; don't stretch yourself too thin by specializing your menu."

Desserts

Ancho Chile Brownies
The Fat Cactus

Banana Pudding
Rollin' Smoke BBQ

Avocado Sorbet
Ice Cream Social

Chocolate-Covered Strawberry Mochi Ice Cream
Fresh Off the Truck

Crema Catalana (Catalan Custard)
Tapas Bravas

Deep-Fried Cinnamon Crunch Muffin with Banana and Nutella
Hey!...You Gonna Eat or What?

Friands
La Boîte Café

Grandma's Sheet Cake Brownies
Tenderland

Funky Monkey Donut
Gourdough's

Grilled Peach with Fresh Rosemary Ice Cream
Ice Cream Social

Lumpia (Sweet Fried Banana Egg Roll)
Be More Pacific

Holy Cacao Diablo Cake Balls on a Stick
Holy Cacao

Holy Cacao Mexican Hot Chocolate
Holy Cacao

Holy Cacao Mexican Frozen Hot Chocolate
Holy Cacao

Holy Cacao S'mores on a Stick
Holy Cacao

Makin' Bacon Sundae
Cow Tipping Creamery

Strawberry Shortcake Smoothie
MamboBerry

Peach Cobbler mmmpanadas
mmmpanadas

Sweet Texas Tea with Mint and Lemon Pops
Ice Cream Social

Ancho Chile Brownies

Courtesy of The Fat Cactus

Spicy, sweet and savory. You haven't had brownies like this before.
Yield: 24 brownies.

1 ¼ cups all-purpose flour

1 teaspoon salt

2 tablespoons dark unsweetened cocoa powder

¾ teaspoon cinnamon

¼ teaspoon cardamom

11 ounces dark chocolate (60 to 72 percent cacao), coarsely chopped

1 cup (2 sticks) unsalted butter, cut into 1-inch pieces

2 ancho chiles stemmed, seeded and soaked in boiling water for 20 minutes and pureed

1 teaspoon instant espresso powder

1 ½ cups granulated sugar

½ cup firmly packed light brown sugar

5 large eggs, at room temperature

2 teaspoons pure vanilla extract

• Preheat the oven to 350°F. Butter the sides and bottom of a 9- by 13-inch glass or light-colored metal baking pan.

• In a medium bowl, whisk the flour, salt, cocoa powder, cinnamon and cardamom together.

• Put the chocolate, butter, ancho puree and instant espresso powder in a large bowl and set it over a saucepan of simmering water, stirring occasionally, until the chocolate and butter are completely melted and smooth. Turn off the heat, but keep the bowl over the water and add the sugars. Whisk until completely combined, then remove the bowl from the pan. The mixture should be room temperature.

• Add 3 eggs to the chocolate mixture and whisk until combined. Add the remaining eggs and whisk until combined. Add the vanilla and stir until combined. Do not overbeat the batter at this stage or your brownies will be cakey.

• Sprinkle the flour mixture over the chocolate mixture. Using a spatula (not a whisk), fold the flour mixture into the chocolate until just a bit of the flour mixture is visible.

• Pour the batter into the prepared pan and smooth the top. Bake in the center of the oven for 30 minutes, rotating the pan halfway through the baking time, until a toothpick inserted into the center of the brownies comes out with a few moist crumbs sticking to it. Let the brownies cool completely, then cut them into squares and serve.

Banana Pudding

Courtesy of Rollin' Smoke BBQ

Banana pudding is the perfect dessert after a big BBQ meal. This recipe can be easily doubled or even tripled.

1 (14-ounce) can Eagle Brand Sweetened Condensed Milk

1½ cups cold water

1 (3½-ounce) package instant vanilla pudding

2 cups heavy whipping cream, whipped

36 medium bananas, sliced (dip in lemon juice, if you like)

6 vanilla wafers (1 box)

container of Cool Whip

- In a large mixing bowl, combine condensed milk and water. Add in pudding mix and beat until well blended. Chill mixture for about 20 minutes. Fold in heavy whipped cream into the pudding mixture.

- Layer pudding mixture, bananas and vanilla wafers into a large bowl. Continue layering until you end with the pudding mixture on top. Top off with Cool Whip and crumble remaining vanilla wafers on top.

Rollin' Smoke BBQ, Tony Hamilton

BBQ is a family tradition for Tony Hamilton. His father had always BBQ'd, and his grandfather owns two BBQ restaurants in Kileen (Maurice's). "I got into BBQ-ing when I was a kid. I just got into cooking and grilling and have been BBQ-ing since I was seventeen years old," Tony shares.

Originally from Austin, owner Tony enjoys having his trailer business be in the heart of downtown Austin. Being right next to the popular music venue of Antone's, he feeds a lot of bands. He also serves a lot of football players who have gone to the league: Cedric Benson, Chykie Brown and Derrick Johnson, to name a few. His food is so good he sells out every Friday and Saturday. "I have it down to a science of how many people I'm serving. I cook everything fresh. I don't like having leftover food, so I give any leftovers to the homeless," says Tony. His bestseller is the Playboy sandwich, which piles brisket, pulled pork and sausage all chopped together and smothered with pickles, onions and BBQ sauce.

Avocado Sorbet

Courtesy of Ice Cream Social

Healthy and quick, this dish will fill you up with beautiful natural fats and layers of flavor. This recipe is easy to cater to your own taste preferences: add more coconut milk to make it creamier or more agave nectar to sweeten it up.

1 large organic Hass avocado

fresh lime juice

3 tablespoons coconut milk

fresh cilantro, a few pinches to taste

agave nectar, to taste

coarse sea salt and lime wedge to garnish

• Slice one large organic Hass avocado and place in a sealable sandwich baggie with a generous drizzle of fresh lime juice. Place in freezer until solid. In a blender, mix together the frozen avocado, quality coconut milk (11 grams of fat or higher), a few pinches of fresh cilantro to taste and a nice drizzle of agave nectar. Blend well. Serve in a dish with a side of coarse sea salt and a lime wedge.

Ice Cream Social, Meredith and Lee Dockery

Growing up in Dallas, brother-and-sister team Lee and Meredith Dockery had been working in the restaurant business for all of their adult lives before they decided to start dishing out artisanal ice cream from a custom-outfitted school bus. "We were ready to branch out on our own, both creatively and financially. We needed to prove to ourselves that we could stand on our own two culinary feet and prove to the community that we had something different for them. Something that would open their eyes up to a new side of ice cream," shares Lee.

"We don't have any family history with ice cream, other than fond memories of making it with our mom as kids. We just knew that after so many years in a hot kitchen, it was time to chill out a little bit. Artisanal ice cream seemed like it was right up Austin's alley, and we weren't seeing it mobile, so we jumped on it. There were many frightening batches before we perfected our recipe, but it was well worth it. Strawberry Basil was not a winner, by the way," Lee continues.

"We like clean ingredients, so most of what we use is high quality, organic and locally sourced when possible. We add coconut milk to almost everything so our products are extra creamy with a delicious natural fattiness," explains Meredith.

The Salted Caramel Ice Cream is the Ice Cream Social's bestseller, followed closely by the Peanut Butter Mole. But Meredith's favorite item on the menu is their Tres Leches Ice Cream in a dark chocolate–dipped waffle cone rolled in cardamom-toasted coconut, topped with a chocolate-dipped kettle chip and toasted marshmallows. Lee is more of an ice cream purist. He likes a fresh scoop of Roasted Strawberry Cheesecake Ice Cream. No toppings. Just a cup of ice cream. Maybe it's because a simple cup of their ice cream isn't so simple. "We roast our organic strawberries with a little sugar, fresh lemon juice and almond extract to bring out a really strong flavor. Another favorite is our Matcha Green Tea with Orange Blossom Oil Ice Cream," shares Lee.

If those flavor combinations aren't enough to tempt you, they offer Candied Bacon with Blackstrap Molasses and Dark Chocolate Tamari Almond. They suggest pairing their ice creams with a nice imported beer to take it easy and "live the good life."

Chocolate-Covered Strawberry Mochi Ice Cream

Courtesy of Fresh Off the Truck

Mochi Ice Cream is a Japanese dessert made from mochi (pounded sticky rice).

Ice Cream:

2 cups heavy whipping cream

1 cup milk

1 cup sugar, reserve ¼ cup

4 egg yolks

2 cups fresh strawberries, diced small (or your favorite filling)

1 teaspoon vanilla extract

1 teaspoon fresh lemon juice

ice cream maker

Preparing the Ice Cream:

• Combine heavy cream and milk in a double boiler over medium heat. Whisk together ¾ cup sugar and egg yolks in a bowl until the mixture becomes thick. Slowly temper the yolks by gradually adding milk and cream mixture. Let mixture cool.

• Heat strawberry and reserved sugar in a sauce pot until the strawberry breaks down and becomes syrupy. Add vanilla and lemon juice. Puree in a blender and let cool. Return the mixture to the top of the double boiler and whisk over simmering water until slightly thickened, about 10 minutes. Whisk in strawberry puree, cover and refrigerate overnight.

• Transfer ice cream to the ice cream maker and follow instructions according to manufacturer. Scoop ice cream balls with tablespoon or baller and refreeze while the dough is being made.

Dough:

2 cups mochiko flour (Japanese glutinous rice flour)

2 tablespoons sugar

½ teaspoon salt

1½ cups water

2 tablespoons light corn syrup

3 cups cornstarch for dusting, as needed

round cookie cutter (3-inch)

Preparing the Dough:

• Place first five ingredients in a microwaveable bowl and whisk well. Saran wrap the bowl tightly, but pierce a little hole at the top for ventilation. Microwave on medium for 1 minute.

• With a wet wooden spoon, stir the sticky dough to check for elasticity. Recover and microwave for another minute. The dough will be ready when it turns shiny and smooth.

• With caution (dough is extremely hot) and your wet wooden spoon, turn the dough out onto cornstarch. When the dough cools a little, stretch the dough out using your hands or a rolling pin until the dough is ⅛-inch thin. Dust cutter with cornstarch and cut circles from the dough. Place ice cream balls into center of the dough and pinch your dough upward around the ice cream ball. Freeze for another 30 minutes.

Chocolate Dipping Sauce:

2 cups semisweet chocolate

2 tablespoons shortening

Preparing the Chocolate Dipping Sauce:

• Over a double boiler, melt chocolate and shortening and stir until smooth. Insert toothpick, or using mini tongs, dip the mochi (dough-wrapped ice cream ball) into the chocolate dipping sauce.

• Place on wax paper and let cool until chocolate re-hardens.

Fresh Off the Truck, Paul Mai and Tova Ng

Tova Ng and Paul Mai's concept with Fresh Off the Truck is simple: "We wanted to re-create Asian comfort food with a unique Austin twist. Both Paul and my grandmothers have been cooking in restaurants and for our families all their lives. They have inspired us to create food traditionally with love and to seek to make it original, as you would find it in Asia. We want to bring back that first sensational memory of falling in love when you eat," shares Tova.

Eating fresh is of the utmost importance at Fresh Off the Truck. "Everything is made from scratch, including our breads, pâté, sauces, even down to our teas, which we import from all over Asia. Our meat is freshly roasted and grilled to order. Our motto is Asian Street Food + ATX = Ni-Haowdy. What we mean by that is that we put a little ATX love in our food, whether it comes to size ('cause everything is bigger in Texas) or uniqueness, we want your taste buds to say Ni-Haowdy!" says Tova.

Tova's favorite item on their menu is the Original Banh-mi. It is a Vietnamese French baguette sandwich that contains pâté, Cantonese BBQ pork, pork roulade, cucumbers and pickled carrots and daikon, with a kick of peppers and freshness of cilantro. Chicken Katsu, Paul's favorite, is a traditional Japanese dish: breaded fried chicken breast on top of rice. "We serve ours with a side of macaroni salad for the Hawaiian influence we experienced on the islands, which we felt complemented the dish well and gave it a good personality," explains Tova.

The Bruce Lee (Banh Mi or Rice Box) has Cantonese BBQ pork and sausage with a fried egg on top of jasmine rice or in a freshly baked Vietnamese baguette. It is the truck's number-one seller and certainly something any martial arts master would appreciate in Texas.

Crema Catalana (Catalan Custard)

Courtesy of Tapas Bravas

This custard with a candied sugar coating is similar to crème brûlée but healthier and easier to prepare. It is especially popular around Barcelona and in the northeastern region of Cataluña. Crema Catalana reflects Spain's Moorish influence and, like many Spanish desserts, uses exotic flavors such as lemon, cinnamon and nutmeg instead of vanilla.

2 large good-quality sticks of cinnamon

2 cups whole milk

peel of 1 lemon with a bright color, thick peel and no blemishes

4 large egg yolks

7 tablespoons sugar, reserve 3 tablespoons

1½ tablespoons cornstarch

freshly ground nutmeg (optional)

• Place the cinnamon and milk in a saucepan and place over a low flame, allowing it to slowly come to a simmer. While the milk is warming, peel the lemon, then add the peel to the milk. Simmer for twenty to thirty minutes, taking care not to let the milk boil over, then remove from the heat.

• Using a wire whisk, beat the egg yolks with 3 tablespoons of the sugar and the cornstarch. Strain the cinnamon, lemon peel and any separated milk solids from the milk, then whisk a little of the milk into the egg yolks to temper. Add the egg yolk mixture to the milk while stirring, then cook over moderate heat, stirring constantly, until the mixture has thickened and is smooth, about 5 minutes. Remove from the heat as soon as it begins to boil. Pour the custard into four ramekins and chill 1 hour uncovered in the refrigerator, then cover and chill well.

• Before serving, sprinkle a dash of nutmeg and 1 tablespoon of sugar over each ramekin, then use a kitchen torch to caramelize the sugar. Serve immediately.

Deep-Fried Cinnamon Crunch Muffin with Banana and Nutella

Courtesy of Hey!...You Gonna Eat or What?

With classic bold dessert flavors, this will easily become a favorite special treat.

1 Cinnamon Crunch muffin

2 tablespoons Nutella

1 fresh banana

approximately 2 quarts canola oil for deep frying (enough to submerge entire muffin)

powdered sugar for garnish

Batter Ingredients:

1 cup soda water

1 cup all-purpose flour

1 egg

1¾ teaspoons salt

1½ teaspoons baking soda

1 tablespoon extra-virgin olive oil

• Cut Cinnamon Crunch muffin laterally twice (cut the cap off and then cut the base in half laterally). Spread the three pieces out and spread Nutella onto the top surface of the bottom two pieces of the muffin (not the cap). Cut banana into ¼-inch slices and then place 3 to 4 banana slices onto the top of the muffin sections with Nutella spread. Restack the muffin and wrap <u>tightly</u> with plastic wrap and allow it to sit refrigerated for 2 hours.

• In a medium-sized mixing bowl, starting with the soda water, combine all batter ingredients and whisk to a smooth consistency. Refrigerate until ready to use.

• Heat fryer with canola oil to 325°F. Unwrap the muffin and coat with batter on all sides. Gently lower battered muffin into the oil so that the top of the muffin is facing up. Allow the muffin to fry for 1 minute and then flip it upside-down and allow it to fry for 4 more minutes. Remove. Drain on paper towel. Quarter the muffin and serve. Powdered sugar makes a beautiful garnish.

Friands

Courtesy of La Boîte Café

A light little lemon lime cake.
Yield: 12 servings.

6 egg whites

¾ cup almond meal

½ cup flour

2 cups powdered sugar

14 teaspoons melted butter

1 teaspoon lemon extract

½ teaspoon lime extract

zest from one lemon

zest from one lime

butter for greasing pans

• Preheat oven to 400°F. Whip the egg whites until they are frothy, approximately 5 minutes. Sift in the almond meal, flour and powdered sugar. Add in the melted butter.

• Add lemon extract and lime extract, as well as the lemon and lime zest.

• Whip the batter until it is smooth, approximately 10 minutes. Scoop into the greased muffin pan until each cup is ¾ full.

• Put in oven for 10 minutes, rotate and leave in for another 10 minutes. Remove and let cool.

Grandma's Sheet Cake Brownies

Courtesy of Tenderland

"This dessert recipe is from my grandma's cookbook and carries with it fond childhood memories. We give it to customers on occasion. Without fail, those customers return asking for another one of Granny's brownies. She'd get a hoot outta this being published," says Angela Springer.

Brownies:

2 cups flour

2 cups sugar

1 teaspoon baking soda

1 teaspoon salt

1 cup butter

½ cup water

4 tablespoons cocoa

1 teaspoon vanilla

2 eggs

½ cup buttermilk

• Combine flour, sugar, baking soda and salt in mixing bowl.

• In saucepan on low heat, melt butter, water and cocoa, stirring constantly. Bring to a low boil, then immediately take off heat. Add sauce to flour mixture. Mix just until blended. Add vanilla and then eggs, one at a time. Finally, add buttermilk. Mix for 2 minutes on medium speed. Pour into a greased 11- by 16-inch sheet pan. Bake at 365°F for 17 to 20 minutes.

Frosting:

4 cups powdered sugar

½ cup butter

5–6 tablespoons buttermilk

4 tablespoons cocoa

1 teaspoon vanilla

½ cup favorite nuts, optional

• Place powdered sugar in mixing bowl. In saucepan, melt butter, then add buttermilk and cocoa, stirring constantly, until low boil. Remove from heat, then pour over powdered sugar. Mix on low until blended. Add vanilla, then mix on medium speed for 2 minutes. Add nuts if desired.

• Spread warm frosting on warm brownies and let cool before cutting and serving.

Funky Monkey Donut

Courtesy of Gourdough's

The Funky Monkey is top favorite at Gourdough's, and now you can re-create this popular dessert at home.

Donut:

(This is not Gourdough's dough recipe but a good substitute for home use)

1¼ teaspoons active dry yeast

1½ cups warm water (110°F/45°C)

½ cup white sugar

1 teaspoon salt

2 eggs

1 cup evaporated milk

7 cups all-purpose flour

¼ cup shortening

1 quart vegetable oil for frying

• In a large bowl, dissolve yeast in warm water. Add sugar, salt, eggs and evaporated milk and blend well. Mix in four cups of the flour and beat until smooth. Add the shortening and then the remaining three cups of flour. Cover and chill for up to twenty-four hours (three hours will work if you're in a hurry).

• Roll out dough ⅛-inch thick. Use the top of a drinking glass to cut donuts and use a butter knife to cut out a hole or small round container. Fry in 350°F hot oil for about 5 minutes, turning frequently. If donuts do not pop up, oil is not hot enough. Drain onto paper towels.

Caramelized Bananas:

¼ stick butter, cut into small pieces

1 ripe banana

dash cinnamon

granulated sugar

cream cheese icing

brown sugar

• While donut is frying, melt butter over medium-low heat in a large skillet. Cut one whole banana width-wise into half-inch pieces. Place banana pieces into skillet and sprinkle cinnamon and sugar over top. Cook for several minutes until banana sections soften and begin to brown on skillet side (it is best to not move the banana pieces very much so that they brown and caramelize well).

• Carefully flip each banana piece and sprinkle cinnamon and sugar over top again. Repeat cooking process until caramelized.

Assembly:

• Spread cream cheese icing on donut and top it off with the grilled banana pieces. Last but not least, sprinkle the donut and banana pieces with brown sugar. There you have it—a donut worthy of being a treat any time of the day!

Gourdough's, Ryan Palmer and Paula Samford

Gourghdough's owners and real estate company partners Ryan Palmer and Paula Samford stumbled into the trailer food business by luck. "We would have long weekends where we'd be working and show property all day without eating—we'd be starving. [Paula's] mom and grandmom used to make her doughnuts that were simple with cinnamon and sugar. We would make those as an indulgent thing at the house. We started making them for friends and they started suggesting different ideas, and before we knew it we had a notebook full of ideas," shares Ryan.

With over twenty indulgent oversized options to choose from out of the '78 Sovereign Airstream trailer, it's as hard to finish one as it is to pick one out. The Flying Pig is their bestseller. It's the one with bacon and maple syrup icing. Porkey's is another fan favorite, with whipped cream cheese (not sweet), jalapeño jelly and grilled Canadian bacon.

In case you didn't catch the play on words, "Gourdough's" is meant to signify "gourmet dough" while also using the Spanish word *gordo*, which means fat. The couple got their first taste of the food industry when they opened their donut trailer for business during the Austin City Limits Music Festival in October 2009, and Gourdough's remains one of Austin's favorite trailer stops.

Grilled Peach with Fresh Rosemary Ice Cream

Courtesy of Ice Cream Social

This process yields an authentic flavor that can be made with all local ingredients.

6 fresh, local peaches

4–5 branches fresh rosemary

raw honey, enough to drizzle over the peaches

½ cup softened cream cheese

¼ teaspoon fine sea salt

2 cups organic milk, reserving ¼ cup

2½ cups whole cream

3 cups coconut milk (preferably 11 grams of fat or higher), reserve 1 cup

1½ cups organic cane sugar

3 tablespoons Madagascar bourbon vanilla bean paste (found in natural grocery stores)

1 tablespoon pure vanilla extract

2½ tablespoons cornstarch

• Clean 6 fresh, local peaches and slice them about a half-inch thick. Toss those pits. Grill the peach slices until you see those lovely grill marks and a fair amount of char remains on the peaches, approximately 4 minutes or until the flesh is caramelized on each side.

• Take 4 or 5 hearty branches of fresh rosemary and place in an airtight container with the grilled peach slices. Drizzle the peach and rosemary combo with raw honey and place in the refrigerator overnight to steep in its own magic.

• In a small bowl, blend cream cheese and fine sea salt. Set aside to soften.

• In a large pot, bring to a boil: 1¾ cups of organic milk, whole cream, 2 cups of coconut milk, organic cane sugar, Madagascar bourbon vanilla bean paste and pure vanilla extract. Whisk thoroughly and continue to boil for about 5 minutes.

• While the mixture is boiling, puree the grilled peaches in a blender and set aside. Next, finely puree 2 branches' worth of rosemary with 1 cup of coconut milk and set aside. Whisk together cornstarch with ¼ cup of milk until smooth. Then, you guessed it, set it aside!

• Now add the softened cream cheese mixture to the boiling mixture. Whisk briskly until smooth. Continue to boil another minute, then add the cornstarch mixture to the boiling mixture. This will thicken and smooth out the finished product. Next, add the pureed peaches and rosemary coconut milk mixture to the boiling mixture.

• Remove from heat and place in refrigerator until completely cool. Mix in your household ice cream maker according to its instructions. Store the ice cream in the coldest section of your freezer for approximately 5 or 6 hours, until firm. Scoop into a dish and drizzle honey over the top to make a sweet garnish.

Lumpia (Sweet Fried Banana Egg Roll)

Courtesy of Be More Pacific

Think of these as Chinese dessert egg rolls.

12 spring roll wrappers

3 bananas

1½ ounces peanut butter chips

3 ounces chocolate chips

a few pinches of salt

1 egg yolk

1 quart oil for frying

powdered sugar

• Defrost spring roll wrappers. Peel bananas, cut in half, then cut each half lengthwise. Peel off one spring roll wrapper and lay so it's a diamond shape. Place banana slice, flat side down, lengthwise toward the bottom of the spring roll wrapper. Add a couple of peanut butter chips and chocolate chips distributed as evenly as possible, followed by a sprinkle of salt.

• Follow the wrapping technique on the back of the spring roll wrapper package and seal with the egg yolk. Using a small pot, add enough oil so the egg roll will be completely submerged.

• Heat the oil to 325°F. Lightly drop the Lumpia into the oil once the oil reaches temperature. Make sure the Lumpia stays fully submerged (you may want to use a spoon or strainer to hold it down). Fry until the Lumpia is a light golden brown, approximately 2 minutes.

• Lay the cooked Lumpia on a platter that is lined with paper towels to absorb the oil. Sprinkle with powdered sugar.

Holy Cacao Diablo Cake Balls on a Stick

Courtesy of Holy Cacao

Burn, baby, burn: a cream cheese frosting made with ancho chiles and a touch of cayenne blended into chocolate cake, dipped in chocolate and then topped with cayenne and cocoa-toasted walnuts. Holy Cacao makes chocolate cake from scratch with fresh ingredients as described in the recipes below and then dips the cake balls in a special couverture chocolate available through baking suppliers. However, when they were learning to make cake balls, they practiced with Duncan Hines cake mix and Wilton's candy melts; these ingredients work fine for making your own cake balls at home. You will also need popsicle sticks.

Chocolate Cake:

3 cups all-purpose flour

1½ teaspoons salt

¾ teaspoon baking powder

1½ teaspoons baking soda

2⅔ cups sugar

1 cup + 2 tablespoons cocoa

1 cup + 2 tablespoons water

1 cup + 2 tablespoons canola oil

5 large eggs

¾ cup water

1½ teaspoons Madagascar vanilla bean paste

• Preheat oven to 350°F. Grease a 13- by 9-inch pan.

• In a large bowl, whisk together flour, salt, baking powder, baking soda, sugar and cocoa. Add 1 cup and 2 tablespoons of water and canola oil. Mix for 1 minute. Add eggs, ¾ cup of water and vanilla. Mix 5 to 6 minutes with a whisk, 3 to 4 minutes with a hand mixer or 2 minutes with a stand mixer.

• Pour the batter into the pan and bake for 30 to 35 minutes or until a cake tester inserted into the cake comes out clean.

Ancho Cream Cheese Frosting:

1 large dried ancho chile

1 cup cream cheese, softened

½ teaspoon cinnamon

½ teaspoon cayenne

½ cup powdered sugar, sifted

2 tablespoons + 2 teaspoons milk

¼ tablespoon Madagascar vanilla bean paste

½ teaspoon lemon juice

• Simmer chile in boiling water for 15 minutes to soften. Remove stem and then puree in food processor with ½ tablespoon of the water it was boiled in. Process softened cream cheese in a food processor until smooth. Add cinnamon, cayenne and powdered sugar and beat until smooth. Then add the pureed pepper, milk, vanilla and lemon juice and again beat until smooth.

Cayenne and Cocoa Toasted Walnuts:

2 cups walnuts

cocoa powder

cayenne powder

• Grind walnuts in food processor. Spread on a baking sheet lined with parchment paper. Dust with cocoa and cayenne and toss to coat evenly. Bake at 325°F for 15 minutes.

• Now the fun and messy part begins! Clean your hands well and dig in. Once the cake has cooled completely, crumble it into a large bowl. Add frosting, 1 tablespoon at a time, and press it into the cake crumbs until a mud consistency is reached (there will be frosting left over).

• To make the balls: use a small #40 ice cream scooper or a tablespoon to measure a cake mixture amount. Roll the cake mixture into golf ball–sized balls and place them on a cookie sheet lined with parchment paper. Line a second cookie sheet with parchment paper and place a flat layer of the walnuts on it.

• Melt Wilton's chocolate melts (dark chocolate) in microwave according to package directions. Dip half an inch of the popsicle sticks into melting chocolate and then stick them into the cake balls. Once the chocolate holding the stick into the ball has dried, it is time to dip the entire ball into the melted chocolate and gently shake off excess chocolate. Sit the ball onto the topping. After the chocolate has dried, the cake balls are ready to serve!

Holy Cacao, Ellen Kinsey and John Spilliards

After dating for three months, Ellen and John decided to go into the cake ball business together. But when Ellen told John she wanted to include hot chocolate as a big part of their menu, John thought the triple-digit heat of Austin might not be the place to serve a heated drink. "Ben and Jerry make ice cream in Vermont," Ellen pointed out. So hot chocolate and, more importantly, frozen hot chocolate made the cut.

   With their leftover cake balls, they make "cake shakes," which are milkshakes made with ice cream and cake scraps. Red Velvet Cake Balls remain Holy Cacao's bestseller, but they have other popular flavors too. For example, John's personal favorite is the Brass Peanut Butter, which has actual Nutter Butters inside. From carrot cake to wedding cake, each cake ball is moist and delicious. They make a great dessert on special occasions or just after a meal.

Holy Cacao Mexican Hot Chocolate

Courtesy of Holy Cacao

1 cup whole milk

1 cup heavy whipping cream

dash of Madagascar bourbon vanilla
(optional)

1 cup bittersweet chocolate chips

1 tablespoon Holy Cacao Mexican Syrup

Holy Cacao Mexican Syrup:

This simple syrup is what we use to make our
Mexican Hot Chocolate and Frozen Mexican
Hot Chocolate. It is also great over ice cream
or mixed into your favorite cocktail!

2 cups water

2 cups sugar

2 ancho chiles

1 tablespoon cinnamon

1 tablespoon cayenne powder (more or less
to suit your desired spice level)

• Bring water and sugar to boil. Add peppers,
cinnamon and cayenne and simmer for 10
minutes. Cool. Strain out chiles and seeds.

Holy Cacao Mexican Hot Chocolate:

• Stir milk, cream and vanilla into pan and
warm over low heat for 5 minutes. Turn heat to
medium and add chocolate. Whisk constantly
for a couple minutes, or until the chocolate has
melted completely. Whisk Holy Cacao Mexican
Syrup into the hot chocolate. Pour and enjoy!

Holy Cacao Mexican Frozen Hot Chocolate

Courtesy of Holy Cacao

Yield: 1 serving. Prep time: 20 minutes.

1 cup Mexican Hot Chocolate (see recipe
above)

1 scoop chocolate ice cream

1 cup ice

• Add the hot chocolate to a blender, followed
by ice cream and then ice. Blend until all
ingredients are well mixed. Pour and enjoy!

Holy Caco S'mores on a Stick

Courtesy of Holy Cacao

> *You haven't had s'mores like this before.*

Marshmallows:

The key to making marshmallows is having an accurate candy thermometer, preferably one that attaches to the side of the pan.

vegetable oil to coat pan

¾ cup cold water

4 envelopes unflavored gelatin

3 cups granulated sugar

1¼ cups light corn syrup

¼ teaspoon salt

¾ cup water

2¼ teaspoons Madagascar vanilla bean paste or flavoring of your choice

S'Mores:

popsicle sticks

2 cups melted chocolate

1 package graham crackers, each cracker broken into fours

• Coat a 7- by 11-inch metal nonstick pan with oil. Put ¾ cup cold water into the bowl of an electric mixer; sprinkle with gelatin and set aside.

• Put granulated sugar, corn syrup, salt and ¾ cup water into a medium saucepan and attach a candy thermometer. Bring mixture to boil while stirring to dissolve sugar. Cook, without stirring, until mixture registers <u>exactly</u> 238°F on a candy thermometer, about 10 minutes.

• Attach bowl with gelatin to mixer fitted with the paddle attachment. Pour hot syrup into gelatin mixture. Gradually raise speed to high; beat until mixture is very stiff, about 12 minutes. Beat in vanilla. Pour into prepared pan and smooth with an offset spatula. Set aside, uncovered, for 3 hours or overnight.

• Unmold marshmallow. Lightly brush a sharp knife with oil, then cut marshmallow into 1-inch squares.

• Stick popsicle stick 1 inch into end of marshmallow. Dip marshmallow into chocolate. Sandwich it between graham crackers and set on parchment paper to dry.

Makin' Bacon Sundae

Courtesy of Cow Tipping Creamery

This sundae started out as a "special" at one of Cow Tipping Creamery's Sunday night socials, and it was such a hit that they added it to their permanent menu. While you could make it with any flavor you want, they feel that a good vanilla bean ice cream will not compete with the toppings but rather complement them instead. At Cow Tipping Creamery, they do artisan soft serve. That being said, you're not going to be able to replicate their ice cream without a professional soft serve machine. Instead, you can use a really good vanilla bean ice cream from your local store or use this tried and true recipe and make your own amazing vanilla bean ice cream as a base for this sundae.

Vanilla Bean Ice Cream:

Yield: 1 quart

2 cups heavy cream

1 cup whole milk

¾ cup sugar

¼ teaspoon salt

1 whole vanilla bean

3 egg yolks

1 teaspoon pure vanilla extract

• At Cow Tipping Creamery, they rotate the vanilla beans they use and soak the actual bean in the dairy after they scrape out the seeds. The Tahitian vanilla bean they use has a nice floral hint, while the Indonesian bourbon bean has a wonderful rich, full-bodied flavor.

• Before you get started… you must freeze your ice cream container for at least 24 hours beforehand, and the ice cream base will need to be refrigerated overnight—so plan ahead.

Infusing the Milk/Cream:

• In a heavy nonreactive saucepan, stir together the cream, milk, half the sugar and salt. Split the vanilla bean lengthwise and use the knife to carefully scrape the seeds from the bean. Add the seeds and the split bean to the pan.

• Put the pan over medium-high heat. When the mixture just begins to bubble around the edges, remove from the heat, cover the pan and let steep for 30 minutes.

Making the Base:

• In a medium heatproof bowl, whisk the yolks just to break them up, then whisk in the remaining sugar until smooth. Set aside.

• Make an ice bath in a large bowl.

• Uncover the cream mixture and put the pan over medium-high heat. When the mixture approaches a bare simmer, reduce the heat to medium.

• Carefully scoop out about ½ cup of the hot cream mixture and, whisking the eggs constantly, add the cream to the bowl with the egg yolks. Using a heatproof rubber spatula, stir the cream in the saucepan as you slowly pour the egg and cream mixture from the bowl back into the pan.

• Cook the mixture carefully over medium heat, stirring constantly, until thickened and it coats the back of a spatula or wooden spoon—about 1 to 2 minutes longer.

• Strain the base through a fine-mesh strainer into a clean container. Set the container in the water–ice bath bowl, being careful not to let water overflow into your ice cream container. Stir ice cream until cool, then remove from ice bath. Cover container with plastic wrap, making sure wrap lies down on top of the ice cream mixture. We recommend you refrigerate the base overnight.

Freezing the Ice Cream:

• Add the vanilla extract to the base and stir until blended.

• Freeze in your ice cream machine according to the manufacturer's instructions. Enjoy right away for soft serve–like consistency, or transfer to a clean container and place in your freezer for at least 4 hours.

Wet Walnuts:

Yield: 1½ cups

Having grown up in New York, my favorite ice cream toping of all time was the "Wet Walnuts." I have not seen this offered anywhere outside of the East Coast and just had to introduce this simple yet amazing topping to our ice cream fans.

1½ cups chopped walnuts
pinch of salt
pinch of allspice (optional)
½ cup pure maple syrup

• In a small skillet, toast the walnuts on medium-high heat, being careful not to burn them. Toss in the salt and allspice and stir to coat.

• Add the maple syrup and heat until it just begins to come to a full boil. Stir for 10 seconds, then remove them from the heat and let cool completely. They will be wet and sticky until cooled.

Baked Maple Bacon:

¾ pound thick-cut smoked bacon (16 slices)
1–2 tablespoons good maple syrup

• Preheat the oven to 400°F.

• Place a baking rack on a sheet pan and arrange the bacon in 1 layer on the baking rack. Bake for 15 to 20 minutes, until the bacon begins to brown. Remove the pan carefully from the oven; there will be hot grease in the pan! Brush the bacon slices with maple syrup and bake for another 3 to 5 minutes, until the bacon is a warm golden brown. Transfer the bacon to a plate lined with paper towels and pat excess.

• Once cooled, coarsely chop bacon and set aside.

Hot Fudge:

Yield: 1 quart...you will want a lot of this and it lasts forever stored covered in the fridge.

1 cup water
1 cup corn syrup
2¼ cups sugar (we use organic brown sugar)
1 cup unsalted butter
½ cup unsweetened cocoa powder (use the best quality you can afford)
½ cup chopped dark chocolate (we use TCHO 60 percent chocolate disks)
2 teaspoons kosher salt
1 tablespoon pure vanilla extract

• In a large, heavy-bottomed, nonreactive saucepan, combine the water, corn syrup, sugar and butter and bring to a boil over medium-high heat until the sugar is dissolved, about 10 minutes.

• In a large heatproof bowl, combine the cocoa powder, chocolate, salt and vanilla. Pour the hot liquid and stir until smooth.

• Just scoop out as much as you want and heat in 5- to 10-second increments in the microwave before pouring over ice cream.

Whipped Cream:

Yield: 2 cups

While you can always use ready-made whipped cream topping, there is nothing like handmade whipped cream on top of your sundae. We always serve fresh whipped cream on the truck. Once whipped, it's best if used immediately but will last up to 8 hours in the fridge. It will separate, so rewhip just before using.

1 cup heavy cream

2 tablespoons sugar (on our truck, we use liquid sugar)

1 teaspoon pure vanilla extract

• Combine all of the ingredients in the bowl of a stand mixer or any deep bowl and refrigerate for at least 15 minutes. Whisk on medium-high speed in your stand mixer or with a hand blender with whisk attachments until light and fluffy and holds a medium to firm peak when you lift the whisk out of the bowl, 2 to 3 minutes.

Assembly:

• Put a large serving of Vanilla Bean Ice Cream in a bowl. Add a large scoop, about ¼ cup, of Wet Walnuts. Pour the Hot Fudge over the top of ice cream and walnuts. Sprinkle bacon on top. Add a large dollop of whipped cream and a few more pieces of bacon on top for the "wow" factor.

Cow Tipping Creamery, Corey and Tim Sorenson

The Cow Tipping Creamery is a family-owned business that is dishing up artisan soft serve with decadent handmade sauces and toppings. Before Corey and Tim were making ice cream, she was a dental assistant and he worked at Pixar Animation and Flyrite Choppers. "We had always been fans of food trucks. Then we watched the television series *The Great Food Truck Race*, and we instantly fell in love with the idea of starting a food truck," shares Corey. "This is the hardest and the most rewarding thing we have ever ventured in. We hope to create a legacy for our children and a happy place for our community."

A favorite item on the menu has to be their specialty cone the High Tea. It consists of Vanilla Bean Ice Cream, English lemon curd with crushed tea biscuits and honey dust and topped off with their truck-made whipped cream.

The story of purchasing their truck is a good one. Corey shares, "We knew we wanted a vintage look, but when we started researching old ice cream trucks, the prices were way out of our range. We expanded our search to any pre-'80s step vans. We came across a 1978 retired emergency vehicle for sale in the rural part of Illinois, about four hours from Chicago. We bought it from the pictures on the Internet. Tim then rented a car and made the drive up into the middle of Illinois. After dropping off the rental, he met the seller and was driven another hour to the middle of nowhere. As he drove further into the country, all Tim could think about was every horror movie he'd seen that started off with an innocent car ride with a stranger. There in a field in its entire red-and-white splendor was our truck. Inside was rough and filled with a bunch of boxes and rescue equipment storage. The seller informed Tim that he had checked all the fluids and that the truck should be able to make the thousand-mile-plus journey. '*Should*' make the journey rang in his ears as he drove away. Three days and thirteen hundred miles later and the truck was parked in our Austin, Texas drive. Six months of gutting, painting, fabricating, wrapping and we were ready to open."

Strawberry Shortcake Smoothie

Courtesy of MamboBerry

Ooh la la! This smoothie is based on the strawberry shortcake dessert and includes Nilla wafers.

1 cup ice

4 ounces tart frozen yogurt

1 cup fresh or frozen strawberries

4 ounces vanilla soy (can substitute regular milk)

2 ounces orange juice

½ teaspoon fresh lemon juice

¾ teaspoon pure vanilla extract

6 Nilla wafers

sweeten to taste if desired

• Add ingredients to blender. Blend. Pour. Drink.

Peach Cobbler mmmpanadas

Courtesy of mmmpanadas

A peachy treat to devour with a scoop of ice cream.

1 pound fresh peeled pitted sliced peaches

1 tablespoon white granulated sugar

1 tablespoon brown sugar

1 teaspoon ground cinnamon

1 tablespoon cornstarch

2 tablespoons water

1 package phyllo dough

4 eggs, gently beaten

4 tablespoons cinnamon-sugar mix

• Preheat oven to 350°F. Combine peaches, sugars and cinnamon in sauce pan over medium heat. Bring peach mixture to a simmer. Dilute cornstarch in water in a small bowl. Once peach mixture begins to bubble, temper in cornstarch/water dilution, stirring continuously. Remove peaches from heat once the mixture thickens and peaches begin to break apart. Let filling cool completely.

• Unroll phyllo dough on lightly floured surface. Using a 4-inch cookie cutter, cut out approximately 16 circles. Spoon 2 level teaspoons of the peach filling in the center of the circle. Moisten edge with water. Fold half of dough over filling to make half moon shape. Crimp edges with fork to seal. Repeat with remaining dough and filling.

• Place 1 inch apart on baking sheet. Brush egg wash over each mmmpanada and sprinkle with cinnamon-sugar mixture. Bake mmmpanadas at 350°F for 12 to 15 minutes. Let mmmpanadas cool on rack for 15 minutes.

mmmpanadas, Cody and Kristen Fields

Cody Fields was building wastewater treatment plants in Costa Rica. While in Central America, he discovered a love for empanadas that would later turn into a full-blown food truck business for him and his wife, Kristen. Upon returning to the States, the couple stumbled into their mmmpanada business after an afternoon at a local bar. The bar owner had made plans with another empanada maker to sell at the bar. Since those plans had fallen through, Cody and Kristen saw it as the perfect opportunity to try their hand at a business that would give them more time together while being able to share a food they both loved. The next day, the couple made six dozen of their first batch of mmmpanadas and brought them to the bar owner. A few months later, they bought a food truck with a credit card and they were in the empanada business.

The traditional Argentinian Beef mmmpanada and the Green Chile Chicken are two fan favorites. Other popular flavors are their Spicy Black Bean and the Ham and Cheese.

Mmmpanadas is unique from most food trailer businesses in Austin. The truck is not their sole source of income; they are using the truck as an avenue to promote their product, which they have successfully sold to several grocery stores.

Sweet Texas Tea with Mint and Lemon Pops

Courtesy of Ice Cream Social

Remember that the freezing process diminishes the sweetness of a recipe, so the more honey, the better!

8 cups water

5 tea bags, organic black tea

2 cups organic cane sugar

1 cup raw honey

handful of fresh mint, to taste

3–4 large lemons, thinly sliced into wedges

• In a large pot, boil water and add the tea bags. Boil for another minute, then remove from heat to steep, covered, for about 10 minutes. Discard tea bags and add cane sugar and raw honey. Simmer on low for several minutes until sugar has dissolved.

• Chop a handful of fresh mint and add most of it to the tea. Let tea cool. In a popsicle mold, place one lemon wedge and a sprinkle of the remaining mint in each popsicle compartment. With a baster, add cooled tea mixture to the mold. Place in the freezer for approximately 2 hours (or until the pops are solid enough to hold a popsicle stick upright but not so solid that you have to force the stick in). Once sticks are added and standing upright, freeze pops for another 2 to 3 hours. When ready to serve, let the molds thaw for about 5 minutes, then remove the pops from their compartments.

Index

About the Author

Serving up the American dream one plate at a time, Tiffany Harelik (rhymes with garlic) is a travel and food writer with a focus on iconic street food culture. An avid cook and entertainer, Tiffany is rumored to make the best fried chicken south of the Mason-Dixon. She is also passionate about the American dream, equestrian sports and the great outdoors. Joined by her best friend and food truck entrepreneur Maurine Winkley, the girls put on their aprons to add jams and sauces to the *Trailer Food Diaries* collection.

Visit us at
www.historypress.net